AIM

A I M
THE WORKBOOK

Peter S. Rhodes

J. Appleseed & Co.
San Francisco

CONTENTS

FOREWARD   *ix*

1 IMPRISONED IN THE LOVE OF SELF   1

2 ASLEEP TO THE SPIRITUAL WORLD   17

3 KNOWLEDGE AND BEING   29

4 REMEMBERING OURSELVES   37

5 CHOOSING NEVER TO EXPRESS A NEGATIVE   45

6 LETTING GO OF IDENTIFICATION   53

7 "MINDING" OUR SMALL "I'S"   65

8 TRUE CONSCIENCE AND SPIRITUAL GROWTH   69

9 THE WHOLE NINE STEPS   79

10 SHORT-FORM REPENTANCE, OR WHAT   89
   THE PROPRIUM DOESN'T KNOW   89

11 ENTERING THE UPPER ROOM   99

12 THE "BRING YOUR OWN" CLASS   109

13 TRANQUIL ANXIETY   121

14 TOWARD A HEAVENLY PROPRIUM   131

15 LEST WE BE DELIVERED   139

16 FROM KNOWLEDGE TO EXPERIENCE   149

GLOSSARY   159

ABOUT THE PUBLISHER   164

COVER ART

Deliver Us From Evil. Plaster sculpture by John Flaxman (1755-1826), England, c.1805.

Courtesy of the Glencairn Museum, Academy of the New Church, Bryn Athyn, PA 19009-0757. Photo by Barry Halkin. Cover design/art by Sara A. Hodgson & Ginger DiMaio.

John Flaxman's religious beliefs were strongly rooted in the writings of Emanuel Swedenborg. This sculpture depicts two good spirits and two evil ones struggling over the soul of a person. The rendering of the soul as a human, fully grown adult was unusual in that period and characteristic of Flaxman's work. He may have read the following — or a related passage — when creating the sculpture:

> ...no one can be regenerated unless he also undergoes temptations... In temptation the person is brought into a state in which the evil that possesses him, that is, possesses his own essential self, is dominant. Once he enters this state, evil and hellish spirits surround him, and when they realize that inwardly he is protected by angels those evil spirits reactivate the false ideas he has previously contemplated and evil deeds he has committed. But the angels defend him from within... a battle is taking place at such a time over that person and his eternal salvation, with both sides using what is within him; for

both draw on what resides with the person and
engage in conflict over it

Emanuel Swedenborg, excerpted
from Arcana Celestia 5036(2)

A question often asked about this work is the
following: of the five people and one serpent in this
sculpture which are good and which evil?

Stephen Morley
Director, Glencairn Museum

FOREWARD

The occasion was a summer camp in western Pennsylvania in August, 1976. I sat in the recreation hall with the other campers and watched as a slightly-built man walked in carrying a meat cleaver of impressive size. He looked nervous. He had never expected to find himself in the role of lecturer at summer camp — he was more interested in studying than in lecturing.

The suspenseful atmosphere generated by the meat cleaver grew even more excited only a few minutes into the man's talk, when he lifted the cleaver, swung around, and buried it deep into an old board that was leaning against the wall behind him. The crowd of campers shuddered at the great thud. Then the speaker made his point: we must divide our consciousness if we are to grow spiritually. It was a moment none of us would forget. It marked a kind of dividing-line in our consciousness.

Following the three lectures he gave that summer on the work of Gurdjieff, Ouspensky, and Nicoll, the man — Peter Rhodes — was persuaded to present a series of talks in Bryn Athyn, Pennsylvania. Those lectures were taped. The meat cleaver had seized my attention, and I listened intently to those tapes, from which emerged the original book *Aim*, and now the present volume.

Somewhat later, the congregation in Tucson, Arizona, of which I was pastor, decided to develop a program to support people in their spiritual lives. After considering several approaches, we decided to build on Peter's lectures, especially the use of tasks. My wife, Louise, spent time with Peter, going over the principles he had outlined in his talks. We developed a preliminary discussion program built around twelve tasks.

The pilot program that we began in 1988 not only has continued to the present, but has spread to many other places around the world. We have witnessed tremendous changes in people's lives as they work through the tasks, beginning with the division of attention that was emphasized so dramatically when that cleaver hit the plank.

This book provides further instruction and inspiration in our most basic challenge: continued cooperation in our own spiritual growth. I am delighted to see it in print.

Frank S. Rose
Tucson, March, 1994

IMPRISONED IN THE LOVE OF SELF

Our subject is "we cannot do," meaning that we actually do not have the power to do as we may think possible for us to do. For instance, we may go to church and hear that we are to love our neighbor as ourself, and we think, "Oh, yes." We understand that living the commandment would be a good idea, but really we haven't even recognized that we are *not* living it. We can see how far our usual state is from that of loving our neighbor when we make efforts to live the commandment. It is then that we find out how different we are from what we believe to be true about ourselves. When we make efforts, we recognize that the way we are living our lives is not the ideal. We see the way we treat people internally. *Matthew* tells us:

> You have heard that it has been said, "You shall love your neighbor and hate your enemy," but I say to you, Love your enemy, bless them that curse you, do good to them that hate you, pray for them that do spitefully use you and persecute you, that you may be the children of your Father which is in heaven, for He makes his sun to rise on the evil and on the good, and sends rain on the just and on the unjust. For if you love those that love you, what reward have you? Do not even the publicans do the same? And if you salute your brethren only, what do you more than others? Do not even the publicans do so? Therefore be perfect, just as your Father which is in heaven is perfect. (5:43-48)

I believe that the "publicans" referred to in this passage represent states in us, the hereditary states that value most those people who are like us. But what reward is there if that is how we treat people? When we salute our brother, don't we do that from our proprium, automatically? What reward do we have if we just live mechanically, doing what we do automatically?

In this passage, we are being told to be different, to be like our Lord. We pray, "Thy will be done," but to do God's will, we have to open up to something higher than our usual state, and it is possible to open ourselves up to higher influences only if we can respond from something beyond the publicans in us, with something beyond our natural, proprial way of reacting. I think that is what the passage is talking about, and that certainly is what the Work is about.

Here is Maurice Nicoll, in *Psychological Commentaries on the Teachings of Gurdjieff and Ouspensky*, on not identifying with the publicans, or negative states, in ourselves:

> The main key lies in preventing one's loss of force through not identifying. There are certain trains of thoughts, for instance, that cause loss of force. It may take some years before you see why. And it often happens that things you think about, and thought were quite harmless and even admirable, will cause great loss of force. So one gains force by every act of non-identification because one prevents its loss and creates force by self-remembering.

Nicoll also quotes Gurdjieff, the Russian philosopher. Now, Gurdjieff was not very pleasant when talking about the nature of humanity, so we should remember that he is talking here about the proprium and the nature of our many different "I's," or states — he is not talking about us.:

> Man's chief delusion is the conviction that he can do. All people think that they can do; all people want to do. The first question all people ask is what are they to do, but actually nobody does anything and nobody can do anything. This is the first thing that must be understood.... Out of himself a man cannot produce one single thought nor one single action. To establish this fact for oneself, to understand it, to be convinced of its truth, means getting rid of a thousand illusions about

man. It is the most offensive and unpleasant thing you can tell people. It is particularly unpleasant because it is true and nobody wants to know the truth.

We cannot do. It is very important that we give up our illusions, one of which is that we can do something active. The truth is that all we can do is let the Lord do something within us.

We know that there is a difference between being and knowledge. We know that we can know certain things. For instance, I know that I shouldn't eat certain foods, but sometimes I eat them anyway. I know that I should walk a certain amount for my heart. Well, I don't do it. There are a lot of things I know I should do that I don't, and a lot of things I know I shouldn't do that I do. So, we know that our knowledge can be far beyond our being. When the Work asserts that "man cannot do," it refers to our being's ability to will and to do and to act in freedom at our present stage of development.

Nicoll talks about the seven levels of a person's transformation. He sees the story of creation not as the creation of the world or of the natural person, but as the creation of the spiritual person. On levels one, two and three, he says, are people who don't have freedom. A person at level one is living from the instinctive center, instinctively seeking those things that give physical gratification. A person at level two is an emotional person, the artist, the sentimentalist who is run by feelings. A person at level three is the intellectual, the left-brain person who is run by the mind. None of these people can do. They respond to life, or external influences, from their proprium. Impressions of things that happen in the external world go into their proprium, into their love of self, and they respond from tendencies they have inherited. They are just like machines, without free choice. Their responses come from their parents and from their upbringings.

If I bumped into each of a hundred different people as I walked around a corner, I could pretty well predict their internal response. Externally, some of them would be very nice to me, while others might punch me. But internally, the response would likely be, "You stupid so-and-so..." They would respond mechanically, and their response would come so fast, so automatically, that they wouldn't have any freedom in that moment to make a choice.

Where does freedom start? Freedom starts at level four. At level four, we act from conscience and with self-awareness. Before that, we are the darkness and the void. We are the living dead before the division of light from darkness takes place at level four. Before the Lord breathes life into us at level seven, before we are spiritually free at levels five and six, we are just starting to see the difference between night and day, but we are not yet free. Most of us are trying to become a level-four person of conscience and awareness. We aren't there yet, but level four is our present goal and hope.

Freedom is not on levels one, two or three of humanity's development. It is possible at level four. At our present stage, the proprium is active and it has to become passive. As long as the proprium is active, we are not free. When the essence, or the new will, becomes active, then we can be free. We know that we are vessels; we are not the source of life, we just receive life. In Swedenborg's *Arcana Celestia*, some angels talk to spirits, asking them where they think life comes from. There are spirits who think that they produce their own life, so the angels do a little experiment, slowing influx to show the spirits how much of their life comes from themselves, which is *none of it*.

Coming to love our neighbor is a long, slow journey, and before the journey starts, we must allow the Lord to remove the love of self that holds us prisoner. A metaphor for this transition might be the children of Israel enslaved in Egypt. Certainly, the children of Israel weren't free to leave Egypt. They were slaves. If they went to Pharaoh one day and said, "You know, we don't like it here and we're leaving," he wouldn't just let them go. They had a long struggle with Pharaoh.

We can picture how it might have been for those imprisoned slaves in Egypt. There might be old prisoners as well as new, young ones. A new, young prisoner might say to a seasoned, old prisoner, "Hey, this is terrible! Let's get out of here! We've got to leave. I'm not going to put up with them telling me what to do. I'm going to break out!"

The old prisoner probably would say, "Hey, you try to get out of here and they're going to kill you. You've got to study things for a while and get some information about the setup. Don't make any hasty moves. First, find out where all the walls and gates are and learn the guards' habits."

The young ones thus might start trying to acquire the information needed to gain their freedom. But it would take time, and after a while, one of them might graduate from latrine-cleaning to the laundry. It's nice and warm in there and she gets free clothes. A little later, they give her a job in the kitchen, where she can even eat what she wants. Then, she graduates to a single-bunk cell and the guards start to put her in charge of other groups of prisoners. Occasionally, she's allowed to go out into the community to run errands. Things seem to be getting better. Now, does this person want to escape?

Eventually, a new, young prisoner comes to such an older prisoner and says, "Let's break out now!" But the older prisoner might now answer, "Just hold on — I don't know about that. Things aren't so bad. I'm not real sure I want to break free now. If I do break, I could get killed or be worse off than I was in the beginning. I've worked a long time to get where I am."

A lot of the children of Israel didn't want to leave Egypt. Similarly, a lot of our states of mind don't want to leave love of self and go to love of our neighbor. The fact that our spiritual side is held captive, like the children of Israel, does not mean that it wants to be free. It appears that Moses, who was raised by Pharaoh's daughter, had a pretty good life. He had to see his people being seriously abused before he began to think, "I'm not an Egyptian. I want us to get out of here." Then, when he went to tell Pharaoh that they were leaving, he was told that they could not.

Things had to get really bad for Pharaoh, too, before he would let the children of Israel go. We have to see our natural lives in a mess and feel some real pain, for ourselves and for those we love, before we are willing to do the Work and let the Lord change us. We have to realize that we are captives, that we are in prison and that things are bad. When the plagues started making Pharaoh's life miserable enough, then he began to consider letting the children of Israel go. When our natural lives produce enough pain for us, then we consider means of escape.

Where are we? Have we already broken out of Egypt? Or are we still making bricks with straw? Are we captive to negative states from hell? Are we still making our own ideas, our own likes and dislikes, opinions and judgments? Or are we free? I suggest that at its present level of spiritual development, humanity is not free. We are coming to a point of freedom, but we are not free in the way that we can be, eventually.

Through self-observation, we find that we are not free. We may find, for instance, that we are not free to like someone whom we dislike, even though we have learned not to act from that dislike. Or, we may decide that we want to give up reacting with anger to our children, but find that we are not yet free to do that, that we are still slaves to those states. Or, we may say to ourselves, "I'm not going to talk behind people's backs because I know that isn't right." The next thing we know, that evil spirit is with us, and we are talking behind someone's back again. Are we free or aren't we free?

We cannot do, but we must do what we can.

What can we do? Fortunately, the Lord separated the will and the understanding. If the will and the understanding were one, there would be no hope. We would be slaves forever and we could not regenerate; our will would be evil and our understanding would be joined to it and there would be no hope. When the Lord made the division between the will and the understanding, it became possible for humanity to change. The Lord says that we can elevate our understanding, that we can elevate our rationality, and that we can look down on the nature of our will. When we look down on the nature of our will through doctrine, through what the Lord says, we perceive things in ourselves that we don't like. We see that the spiritual parts of us, the very parts that should be in charge, are slaves. And we dislike that and wish for something different. When that wish is strong enough, we want to break free. But life is not going to be easy even then, because once we get out of Egypt, we still have a long journey ahead of us.

There is a space — after we leave Egypt but have not yet arrived in the Promised Land — between an active proprial state and the love of doing good toward our neighbor. In that space, there is an empty feeling. We don't have the delights of Egypt: we are not allowed to talk behind people's backs, we are not allowed to wallow in our negative emotions, and we are not allowed to enjoy our internal dialogue and our lying. We are asked to give up the things that we used to enjoy so much, but we don't yet have love of the neighbor, love of use, love to the Lord, or any of the things that will replace the negatives, so we come to an empty space. When we experience that emptiness, our tendency is to fill it quickly with some new excitement.

However, we must be patient. There actually is a quality to that empty space in itself. Imagine a house full of teenagers, playing their discs and the T.V. and touch football in the living room, all at the same time. If, suddenly, they all went out to a movie, we would certainly notice the emptiness in the house, but also a certain quality to that emptiness that is pleasurable. Likewise, when we start to get some distance from our mean, petty "I's," there is an initial emptiness, but there is also a quality of goodness to it. I think it is comparable to manna; it has a very light, subtle, honey-like taste. If we pay attention to where we are, compared to where we have been, we will see that the emptiness has an affirmative quality. There is enough manna in that state to get us through to the next day.

The question arises whether this state of emptiness is like the swept and clean house in *Luke* 11:24-26:

> When an unclean spirit goes out of a man, he goes through dry places, seeking rest; and finding none, he says, "I will return to my house from which I came." And when he comes, he finds it swept and put in order. Then he goes and takes with him seven other spirits more wicked than himself, and they enter and dwell there; and the last state of that man is worse than the first.

The answer is no, in my opinion. In the emptiness between subduing old inclinations and starting new habits, or loves, there is the discontented murmuring of missing the delights of our former state, the food-pots of Egypt. But, if we actually go back to Egypt, things will be much worse than they had ever been before. If we are far enough along in the Work so that we can clearly see the nature of our proprium, and then we quit working to return to the delights of contempt and self-pity, embracing those negative emotions as if we didn't know better, we are in deep trouble. I think the Word is talking about that, the part of us that might really decide to go back to Egypt — our former state of evil — rather than the part that is just fussing about missing it.

If, while working on an evil, we actually do return to Egypt, we do not go back to where we were before we had some success in conquering the evil. We go to the state we would have been in had we been under the hypnotic influence of the hells the entire time. That murmuring part of us that wants, for instance, to "let go" and talk behind people's backs is a common, mild temptation, but the hells want us to embrace the entire falsity of believing, "This old way is really right. This is the way to live."

When, in the Work, we have to give something up, such as the food-pots of Egypt, what we have to give up are its negative aspects, not those aspects that we can use for our regeneration. For instance, the Work tells us that we have to give up personality. It means false personality. But between false personality and personality there are mediate personalities that have a little good and a little bad about them, but are capable of being used. The Writings tell us the same thing: there are states that can be raised and made useful, but there are other states that definitely cannot be used. A negative emotion like contempt cannot be used; we have to give that up. However, consider the part of us that likes to be liked. That is part of false personality, but we can see that being liked is useful in business, at home, and with friends. The desire to be liked can be used to serve regeneration. It is mediate, not evil, so we purify it instead of throwing it out. We see that it can be used for good purposes as well as for selfish ones. If we focus on its good purposes, stay aware and observe as much as we can, there is a gradual change.

Through self-observation, something takes place. It is analogous to someone growing up on the natural plane. Young kids are in ego, seeking gratification. I remember when I was in my twenties, drinking too much, staying up late, passing out — all that sort of behavior. How did I get from there to being forty-three years old, going to bed at nine-thirty, getting up at six, having a briefcase and putting on a tie, telling parolees in my office that they should stop using this and that — how did I get to this? It wasn't because I should have — my teachers were telling me that I "should" long before I changed. It was because I started to look at what was pleasing to me, what was pleasing to my inherited, natural state, or "IT." I started to catch glimpses of the true nature of IT, and when I saw that nature, I didn't like IT so much. I started to dislike those things that I had liked and, gradually, my tastes changed. Gradually, I was led away from what I used to like to something brand new.

In his theological writings, to which we refer as the Writings, Emanuel Swedenborg suggested that if we treat people internally as we do externally, we are pretty far along the path of regeneration. If we have been standing in line for half an hour at the movies when someone rushes up and says, "Sorry, I'm really in a hurry, can I get in front?" we might say, "Oh, sure, go ahead." But, internally, we might not treat such a person the same way. However, if we respond internally as nicely as we do externally, we might be pretty far along on the road of regeneration. The same kind of growth has to take place internally as takes place externally, and that requires something brand new. We have to realize that our internal life is not what we think it is.

Swedenborg talked to different people about how they envisioned their spiritual states. Some people imagined that they were in a lovely field with little lambs running around and butterflies and a stream going by. Swedenborg asked them how their lives were, and they said, "Just great — wonderful." When asked if they would like to see a representation of their lives in the light of heaven, they said that they would. When their lives were seen in the light of heaven, there were snakes, tigers, lions and bears in a miserable desert. What happened? They saw *the way it really is*.

When we draw up into self-observation, we look down on what we think are pretty nice people. I'm a pretty nice guy, right? Well, when we draw ourselves up and look down in the light of the Work and in the light of doctrine, what we see are snakes, lions and bears, and we realize that our usual state isn't so good. We find that we dislike what our proprium, or IT, likes. We dislike the feelings that IT offers us, such as contempt, covetousness, rage and self-pity. We dislike them, but we also find that we are slaves to those states, imprisoned in them, and we dislike that, too. However, we are not yet free to leave. As slaves in Egypt, the children of Israel couldn't just go up to Pharaoh and say, "I saw you beating someone — I'm leaving," because Pharaoh would kill them. The first thing to do is to observe ourselves — observe our behavior, our thoughts and our feelings. Something starts to change with that observation.

If we suppose that we already have freedom and rationality, we are supposing that we have a great deal. Perhaps we don't have them at all. Perhaps we have to do a great deal of work before we get to freedom, before we can observe from rationality rather than from the proprium.

In one sense, yes, we are free, but there is work to be done on our negative states, our love of self and our love of the world, before we can utilize the freedom that the Lord has made available to us. When we talk about freedom, we have to know which level of development we are talking about. A person at level four has rationality. A person at level five has freedom. Which person are we? Which stage of development are we in now? When the creation story speaks of dividing the day from the night, we shouldn't assume that we are at the stage in which fruit is falling from our trees. In *Arcana Celestia*, Swedenborg writes:

> By receptacles are meant the very forms of men. For men are nothing else than the forms receptive of life from the Lord and these forms are such by inheritance and by their actual life that they refuse to admit spiritual life which is from the Lord. But when these receptacles have been so far renounced that they no longer have any freedom from man's own, then there is total submission. A man who is being regenerated is at last so far reduced by repeated alterations of desolation and sustenance that he no longer wills to be his own but the Lord's. And when he has become the Lord's he comes into a state of such a nature that when he is left to himself he grieves and is seized with anxiety and when he is delivered from this state of self he returns into his happiness and bliss. (6138)

This indicates to me that the Lord, through a long process of putting each of us in states in which we are controlled by the proprium, and then withdrawing us from those states, brings us eventually to a state in which we can submit ourselves to God. And even then, the Lord will allow us back into our proprium. We may think, "I'm back in my proprium, I must have failed." No, the passage doesn't say that. It says that the Lord will let us back into our proprium and that at some point, we will get sick and tired of being the way that we are in our proprium. We will dislike that state. Then, the Lord withdraws us from that state and makes it quiescent. Then we feel thankful toward the Lord. When we are in our proprium, it is not we who are failing. It is not we who are doing it. Both these states are in the Lord's order. The Lord is making these transitions in us. When we are in the proprium and "cannot do," it does not mean that we choose not to do. It means that God is allowing that experience for us.

The Lord has made the division of our will and our understanding possible. We can look down upon what we see going on in our lives and think about it from the Work, from doctrine and from the rational. We can reflect upon what we see below. But if we are thinking from the natural and the appearance, we may think, "That person ran over my cat and I'm angry." We blame others for our anger and attribute everything to natural causes. We feel that we are the state that we are in, rather than being aware of the influx from hell or heaven that is acting through us. If we think from the appearance, we are not aware of influx from the higher societies in heaven. We can elevate our mind into the rational if we will, and only then can we comprehend higher influences. Swedenborg writes of our unawareness in *Apocalypse Explained*

> Some angels of the lowest heaven who did not comprehend that evil and falsity are from hell, because they had believed in the world that they were themselves in evils from birth and from actual life, were led through infernal societies and in each one they thought just as the devils thought in that society. They were told to think from themselves and thus otherwise, but they said that they were wholly unable to do so. In this way they were made to comprehend that evils and falsities flow in from hell. All this makes clear that the quality of each one's life flows in from without. With regard to myself I can testify that for fifteen years I have clearly perceived that I have thought nothing and willed nothing of myself, also that every evil and every falsity has flowed in from infernal societies and every good and truth has flowed in from the Lord. (1147)

We can see that Swedenborg is having influx from hell. He is having thoughts from hell and he is having feelings from hell. However, he perceives that the influx is from hell. It is not as if Swedenborg didn't have that experience of evil; he did, but he saw it for what it was. He saw that it was from hell, rather than justifying it or rationalizing it. We are given that same ability to raise our minds into the rational, to see where our thoughts and our feelings are coming from.

Therefore, we will observe ourselves. We will raise our rational into the light of heaven and the Work. Our task is to observe something in our thoughts and in our feelings. We may think that we are running around in a lovely field filled with little sheep, goats and butterflies, but we will find that is not true. We will observe what is really in our field. The task is simple: it is to observe our lying. We will observe that our proprium is a liar.

We want to observe lying of two types. There is lying such as saying, "Boy, did I tell off that guy at the garage today!" when we actually meekly said, "Sir, may I have my car?" There is also the kind of lying in which we talk about something that we know nothing about as if we do know about it. We, who have never met a politician in our lives, hear ourselves expressing an opinion of one. Or, we are more than happy to tell others why a certain judge should not be on the Supreme Court, even though we may know nothing about it. Let us just observe such lying in ourselves. In *Commentaries*, Nicoll writes of this second type of lying:

> Study man's present state of sleep (which I believe we are in) and you will see it is absence of unity, it is mechanical, and lacking control. We find many wrong functions which are the result of this state, in particular, lying to himself and other people all the time. The psychology of ordinary man could even be called the study of lying, because man lies more than he does anything else. In fact, he cannot tell the truth. It is not so simple to speak the truth. One has to learn how to do it and sometimes it takes a very long time. Lying is thinking or speaking about things that one does not know. This is the beginning of lying. It does not mean intentional lying (which we also do upon occasion) like telling stories such as that there is a bear in the other room, when there isn't, because then you could just go in the other room and see that there is no bear there. But if you collect all the theories that people put forward on given subjects without their knowing anything about it, you will see where lying begins. Man does not know himself. He does not know anything and yet he has theories about everything. Most of these theories are lying.

We will watch for lying, but not because we are lying. IT, the proprium, is lying. If we feel guilt because we lie, we fail to understand that we don't have much chance of doing anything else, because we are not yet free. We are still servants and slaves to the proprium and what we will notice is that the proprium lies. The proprium talks as if IT knows what IT is talking about, although IT doesn't. These are the weasels in our field. We could watch the lions, which represent when we beat up on people and yell at them. We could watch the tigers, when we destroy people behind their backs. We could watch the rats, or the snakes, when we hurt people's feelings. We could look at all these animals in our field. When we raise our rationality up and use self-observation, we don't have to wait very long to see that all the animals we speak of are there in our field, but for now we are just going to look at lying.

When, in conversation with another, we talk about a third person who is not present, there is a great probability that we are lying. There are at least four types of lies that we may find ourselves using in such a triangle:

We may be simply out-and-out lying about the absent third person. There is a tendency for two propriums to bond with each other and then to infer that another person who is not present is wrong in some way. There is a bonding of two propriums in feeling superior to a third. Propriums do that. We tend, in forming threes, to make two against one. In order for two propriums to bond in this way, they must do a certain amount of lying to make it appear that they are right while the third person is wrong. We can observe our proprium doing that.

We also lie by speaking of things we know nothing about. We find ourselves commenting on all sorts of things we know nothing about, such as another's behavior, the problems they are having, why they do what they do, the worth of the decisions they make, or what they did last week.

We also lie by falsely attributing our own states to another's behavior. I may observe myself saying, "When Joe Smith did that, he made me so angry." Such an attitude is not Work-oriented. IT talks as though another person could make me mad. Or, I may make a remark like, "She doesn't do her job. I have to do it for her all the time. It makes my job miserable!" However, her behavior cannot make me miserable. We know from the Work that such a statement is a lie: our misery comes only from within us, from hell. For us to speak as if that were not true is a form of lying.

Finally, we lie when we bring up only what makes us look good and another person look bad. IT is telling only half of the story, the half that makes IT seem good and another person seem bad.

Lying is very hurtful to other people. When I am in court, if I begin my testimony with, "Well, I heard that Harry did..." the judge will say, "Hold on, we don't accept hearsay evidence. Did you actually see Harry do it? If not, then you can't speak on that matter." The judge realizes that I may be lying, and the court wants only first-hand information.

Hearsay is very dangerous. The proprium's justification for hearsay is, "If I hear it, it has to be true." The proprium is even more convinced if IT hears ITSELF say something! The first time the proprium hears ITSELF say something untrue, IT probably knows that there are certain lies involved, but the second time IT hears ITSELF make such a statement, IT is pretty convinced that the lie must be true. The third time IT hears the lie, IT is totally convinced and completely believes the lie. After a while, IT presents the lie to the world as the actual truth.

It is important for us to observe that lying is mechanical, that it takes no effort and no attention, and that IT, our proprium, is often lying, especially when we form a twosome and talk about a third person who is not present.

If we find ourselves lying, we can go ahead and try to stop. We will find that sometimes we can stop and that sometimes we cannot. Sometimes, we will find that we are slaves: if the societies that are with us want us to lie to someone, we may catch ourselves lying in mid-sentence, but find that we still finish the sentence. Sometimes, we will find that we can stop lying in mid-sentence. In our task, we will notice when we actually do have a choice and when we have no choice whatsoever.

If we hear ourselves making a case, sounding like an attorney within ourselves, defending our own bad behavior, bad thoughts or bad feelings, we should be aware that most likely IT is starting with a false premise and is lying. That is another form of lying: rationalizing and justifying with statements that are totally made up and fictitious. We will find a lot of different forms of lying. We even may find that everything we say, to ourselves and to others, is lying. We could choose an easier task: to discover if we tell the truth even once!

When we raise our minds to a higher level and see things in the light of heaven, we see what is. We see the proprium, but that is not us. Swedenborg has told us that, from the Lord. He even said, "It is not me; it is from hell." Rather than feeling that IT is from us, and consequently attempting to justify IT and make IT look good, we will just look at IT and say, "That's not good at all!" There is no point in feeling guilty. If we feel guilty, we start to attribute evil to ourselves, and then it is even harder to separate from IT. We know that we are prone to evils of every kind. We have to find those evils and see them, but not feel guilty about them. Why feel guilty about the way it is? That is just the way the proprium is. But we are going to dislike some of the things that we look at, and that dislike grows the more we look at those things.

The more we catch IT lying, the more we dislike that IT is lying and that IT is using us to lie. We are subservient to liars from evil societies.

We are perverted people: what should be ruling is serving, and what should be serving is ruling. The situation has to be inverted. As we look down and see how we are lying, cheating, stealing and mistreating people, in fact or in our thoughts and our feelings, we develop a distaste for IT. When we get a strong enough distaste for IT, perhaps we will let the Lord create a new will in us. Then that inversion can take place. Then we can be free, rather than slaves to negative spirits acting through us. The children of Israel can be free, rather than slaves to the Egyptians.

THE TASK:

To observe how our proprium lies:

(1) By speaking or thinking untruths;

(2) By talking about things we know nothing about as if we do know;

(3) By justifying, rationalizing, or "making a case" for our position.

2

Asleep to the Spiritual World

Attention is a powerful thing. We can direct our attention. We can pay attention. In *The Fourth Way,* P.D. Ouspensky suggests that a person in church who is using her intellectual center is going to hear an entirely different sermon than another person who might be in his moving, or instinctive, center due to being hungry or tired. The person listening to the sermon with her intellectual center is using intellectual effort and energy to pay attention.

Consider an analogy. If we were lost, we might call up a friend and say, "Look, I'm in Willow Grove and I want to get to Conshohocken." We're on a pay-phone and our friend starts to give us directions. Now, we're going to pay attention to everything said, because if we miss one turn or one route number, we're not going to get there! That is the kind of attention we have to pay when we are talking about a trip from love of self to love of the neighbor, because it is vital information. If we miss one turn, we don't know where we might wind up. We could end up in south Philly rather than Conshohocken. We wouldn't want that, would we?

We see skits about people using drugs who exclaim, "Wow, far out!" as they have insights about insignificant things. It may be that they are really insightful, but when they come down, they forget their insight and it is of no use to them. They may borrow energy to be at a very high center and to see things that we don't usually see. Unfortunately, that energy is stolen from them by the drugs and they have to gain it back later on. However, we can get to a higher level than usual without drugs and hear things in a sermon that we couldn't possibly understand if we were hearing it from a lower level. In *Commentaries,* Nicoll writes:

Gurdjieff used to say that no one realizes his own situation. All of you are in prison and all you can wish for if you are sensible people is to escape. At one time his favorite statement was that if man is in prison and is to have at any time the chance to escape, he must realize first of all that he is in prison. So long as he fails to realize this, and so long as he thinks he is free, he has no chance whatsoever.

Have you taken this day quite mechanically? Have you taken your domestic problems just the way you always have? Have you tried to transform anything by taking it in a new way? It is difficult, but it is possible. This is the supreme object of the Work.

We have talked about how we are in prison, and about how we are mechanical. Another way of understanding where we are is to say that we are asleep. The usefulness of saying that humankind is asleep is that it may be easier to think of waking up than it is to think of not being mechanical, or of not being unconscious, or of the need to break out of prison. We all know what waking up is. We have all been asleep and we have all awakened, so it is pretty clear in our natural lives what it is to wake up. We are not usually asleep in relation to our natural lives. But we are asleep in relation to our spiritual lives. Some examples can show different degrees of natural and spiritual sleep and wakefulness.

Suppose we observe someone lying on a couch. We see that her eyes are closed, her mouth is slightly open and her breathing is heavy. Perhaps her mind is in a dream, flying over the Grand Canyon in Arizona. That is where she is and that is where her attention is, there in Arizona, looking at the mountains and the cactus. If that is where her mind is, but her body is on the couch, we say that she is asleep to natural life. We are standing near her, but she is not awake to that fact. She is asleep to natural life.

Let's say that we come into our house and find that something isn't done that we had expected would be done. The kids didn't clean up, and we start yelling at them, "I told you to clean that mess up. It really makes me angry that you didn't do it!" In the spiritual world, the good spirits who are with us see that suddenly we have left them. We are blaming this event for making us angry, but the good spirits can see that our spirit has moved into a society called love of dominion, and that society is causing us to be angry. We are spiritually sound asleep! We are focused somewhere else, called the natural world, whereas all causes arise in the spiritual world. We are asleep to spiritual life.

Now, let's say that we are in that dream of the Grand Canyon, flying over Arizona. Suddenly, we say to ourselves, "I can't fly — I must be dreaming! I'm really in bed, sound asleep!" However, we are still in the dream. We are dreaming, yet we are aware that we are dreaming. We are therefore a little more awake to where our body is in the natural world. We are asleep, but we are aware, at least, that we are asleep, or rather, that our body is asleep.

Finally, suppose that we observe ourselves getting angry and blaming an external event — the kids not cleaning up — as the cause. But we are aware of the truth that the external is not the cause; the cause is in the spiritual world. We are waking up more to the spiritual reality of what's going on. We are not totally asleep to the spiritual cause of our negative mood. We are now aware, at least, of a spiritual cause. We are aware, at least, of the danger of being asleep on the spiritual level.

We must wake up. But first we need to know that there are different kinds of sleep. If I went into a field and fell asleep, that might not be dangerous. But, if I fell asleep in a field in Africa, it might be very dangerous. If I fell asleep on an old, unused train track after having a few drinks, there might not be a problem. But, if I did the same thing on a frequently used track, there might be a big problem! We must realize that we are in a dangerous kind of sleep. We pay a price for being spiritually asleep.

The Word tells us of the need to awake, the need to keep watch. It also tells us of people who weren't prepared, such as the virgins who didn't have any oil, or the guests invited to the wedding supper who didn't have the proper clothes. At those times, it was too late. Likewise, In my work as a probation officer, I see it happen to my clients. I keep warning them that if they do this or that, they are going to have a violation hearing and possibly go back to jail, but they always think that they have an adequate reason or explanation for their behavior. It is a striking thing to see a person who did not think that it was going to happen suddenly be put in handcuffs and taken away. To see that is to see a person whose answers can no longer affect his life.

Similar things happen in natural life quite often. Someone says to a friend, "You know, you better stop drinking and smoking — it's going to take a toll on your heart." And then, later, the friend has a couple of drinks, runs to catch the phone and has a heart attack. All of a sudden, it is too late, because the fact that smoking and drinking might have a bad effect didn't have a reality to it. It didn't feel real, or as real as the drink or the cigarette felt. That friend was asleep to the reality of the situation.

Let's consider the costs and benefits of spiritual sleep and spiritual wakefulness. The proprium constantly seeks gratification. For example, a child is thinking, "Oh, boy, when Mom gets home, she is going to take me to the amusement park!" The proprium is getting excited about getting on those rides and having a fun, physical experience that will be gratifying. However, when Mom comes home, she says, "No, I am not taking you." Anger comes up — the expected gratification has been interfered with. What gratification does the child have now? Perhaps she has a temper tantrum, a second gratification. We don't think of temper tantrums as gratifying, but self-observation reveals that the proprium takes perverse delight in negative emotions such as anger.

Suppose that I am a mid-level manager. My boss comes to me and says, "Look, I am going to give a presentation to the board tomorrow afternoon. I would like you to have each of your people do a report on the various aspects of marketing. Put it together for me. I want it tomorrow morning."

I tell my people what they have to do. One of them does marketing, one advertising, one accounting, and so forth. As I am coming in to work the next morning, my proprium starts to think about getting this project together and handing it to the boss and the boss saying, "Real good job! This is terrific! Just what I wanted. You are really doing a good job. I'm proud of you and I think you have a mighty good future here." My proprium starts to imagine and to exaggerate. The gratification that IT is anticipating is pride, that good feeling of being liked by my boss. Perhaps also IT feels a little bit of love of the world, like the prospect of a raise.

I go into my office, and there on my desk are the reports, and I am glowing. One, two, three, four, five — but I can't find that sixth report. All of a sudden, my proprium starts to have a feeling of impatience and a little irritation — John Jones's report isn't there. I call his office and am told that John Jones isn't at work today; he's at home.

I call John Jones and ask him, "What's going on? I don't have your report. I have to give it to the boss in half an hour!"

"Look," he says, "I just couldn't get it done. My son was sick and I had to take him to the hospital. I just couldn't get to it."

Bam! I hang up the phone, thinking, "How am I going to get this done? I'll have to cover myself." And a lot of anger comes up.

If I am in the Work, I will observe my negative state. I will make efforts not to be identified, to separate. I will ask, "What gratification was IT looking forward to?" Perhaps it was pride, perhaps love of reputation, that IT wanted and anticipated. But ITs gratification was interfered with by John Jones's failure, and now IT is angry.

Through anger, IT is seeking a second gratification. IT is not going to get the love of reputation that IT wanted. But ITs anger may offer a feeling of superiority. I think, "That stupid guy! If I couldn't get to work because someone was in the hospital, at least I would call with a warning, to give someone else time to do something! Or, I would have gotten another fellow to do it for me. I would have had it on the desk." I am getting the gratification called "contempt of another in comparison with myself," which feels like I am good and he is bad. The negative proprium is reveling in a substitute gratification called superiority to other people.

I might ask myself, "What is the price, or cost? What is the cost if I identify with this negative state of anger?" I might think, "First of all, just on the physical level, my body is going to get tense and my ulcer will start bleeding again and I'm going to get a headache. Then, I'm going to start making excuses and justifications to my boss, and that's not going to make him happy, and I'm going to end up lying to him. I will also alienate one of my workers."

What is happening on the spiritual plane? What is the spiritual cost of identifying with this negative state? The habit of responding automatically to the proprium is becoming more ingrained. I am getting more identified, making the negative emotion more my own. I am becoming more and more mechanical. Every time I identify with a negative emotion, I make it more my own and I become more mechanical. Spiritually, that is the price I am going to pay.

Let's say that I withdraw from my proprium and decide that I am not going to respond from my negative emotion. I decide that I will not be identified. What will I get for that? What is the benefit? I get to be a little more awake. I get to be aware of spiritual causes. Evil spirits and love of dominion, acting through the proprium, are the causes of this anger. So, I separate.

How would things have gone if I had separated before talking to John Jones that morning? Let's say that I felt the anger coming and that I realized that it was a proprial love that was being interfered with.

"John, why didn't you get your report in?"

"My kid was sick. I had to take him to the hospital."

"Your kid is hospitalized? Is he all right?"

"No, they don't know what it is."

"Are they going to be able to help him?"

"Yes, I think so."

"Do you need the rest of the day off?"

"Yeah, I sure could use it."

"Okay, you do that. We'll get someone else to take over. Don't you worry about it. What is important now is to be with your son."

I am observing what's going on. I am holding back the proprium and I am not identifying with IT. I call my boss and tell him that the Jones boy is sick and that I will get the report to him as soon as possible.

A different behavior takes place. What's the benefit? I'm relaxed physically, the ulcer is quiet, and I am establishing a real relationship with my employee. I am also having honest dialogue with my boss. I am starting to behave as if there is something more important than my image and my reputation. All these things are benefits of my not being identified.

What are the costs of my not being identified? I am going to have to sacrifice everything the proprium offered me. I am going to have to sacrifice my love of reputation and my feeling of contempt and my feeling of superiority. If I sacrifice these proprial feelings, a new influence can come into me. But I have to separate myself from the proprium before something new is possible.

Self-observation is necessary in a situation like this. We want to practice nonidentification in a clear, concise way. When we feel a negative emotion, we ask, "What is the gratification IT is seeking? What does my proprium want?" If IT hasn't gotten what IT wanted, we ask, "What gratification is it offering me instead, if I identify with IT?" Then, we identify the feelings that are waiting in the wings: superiority, self-pity, contempt — the delights that the hells enjoy so much. We can also ask, "What is the cost to me?" We really look at what it will cost us if we identify with IT. If we respond from that negative emotion, what price will we pay? We'll be shocked!

As we practice these things, we must be aware that there is a great difference between wanting something and doing the Work necessary to reach that aim. We want to be conscious, to be awake, and to feel peace and tranquillity. If that is what we want, we must realize that the Work necessary to accomplish it requires self-observation and separation. When we experience frustration, we will work on the frustration; when we are impatient about how it is going, we will work on the impatience. Through this process, we realize on a deep level what it really takes for us to be awake and aware, and our efforts are grounded in a real understanding of the Work it takes for us to accomplish our aim.

I heard a sermon about some spirits who were told in the spiritual world about true marriage love. They all wanted it. But when they were told what they would have to do to get it, they became sorrowful and went away. It was the same with the rich man who came to the Lord and asked what he should do to merit heaven, since he had obeyed the commandments from childhood. When the Lord said, "Give up your riches," the rich man went away, sorrowful.

We have lots of enthusiastic personality "I's" telling us that they want to do wonderful things. They are so happy about the prospect of the Work, but they are totally incapable of doing the Work, so we immediately find ourselves with a big aim that we are not accomplishing. But we need not be upset, since it is simply the nature of those active "I's" to have big ideas but zero Work-tolerance. We must not let them discourage us. We must take one little step at a time.

On a mechanical level, it is natural not to want to do the Work. For instance, a couple is in love and decides, "We want to get married." There probably is a part of them that is willing to Work through all it takes to be married, but there is another part that just wants to get married. The part that just wants to get married will make it only through the honeymoon plus three days. The marriage is not going to last if there isn't the other part present, the part that is willing to do whatever Work it takes.

Imagine a couple that wants a child. They have been unable to have one for several years, but, finally, they are expecting. Then, they have a beautiful little baby. We look at their faces and we can see that this baby is everything. There is nothing more important to them than this baby. Then, six weeks later, during the night, when the baby needs to be changed for the third time, how is it? Is this baby still so important? For example, we might hear, "I'm trying to get some sleep!" What's happening? The parents are falling asleep to what is really important. And, it is happening just a little at a time. Negative feelings start piling up, covering over what is important. Little by little, we give in and the proprium gets stronger. Eventually, rather than coming from what we really want, we come from what the proprium wants. We get confused between what we want and what the proprium wants. We think that we are the proprium.

My wife and I spent several hours shopping one day. I was a little impatient because she likes to look more closely at things than I do. I was annoyed, but I didn't say anything. There was another couple nearby, and the man was anxious to get out of there, too. He ran the cart into his wife's heel and said, "You stupid woman, I'm sick and tired of shopping with you." He said exactly what my proprium was saying. The negative spirit in me must have decided, "Well, if this jerk won't say anything out loud, I'll work on that other character there." And what that other man said was an exact rendering of what I would have said if I had said anything!

When we listen to such a couple, we wonder, "Where is their love? What is it hidden under? Is all this anger really about how long they are going to shop today?" If they went to a marriage counselor, the first question they would be asked is, "What do you really want?" The couple might answer, "We want to get back in touch with our love." Well, in order to do that they will have to stop identifying with all their proprial likes and dislikes. They will have to wake up to what's going on in them and to what is ruining their relationship.

Both that man and I were asleep during the shopping trip, and it is our sleep that we are observing. While we were asleep, there was the negative gratification, the benefit, of feeling superior and contemptuous. But there was also a cost to our relationships. In my case, the cost also included a lie: I thought that my wife was being stupid when actually she was shopping carefully and thoughtfully. My proprium lied about the length of our shopping trip being more important than my relationship with the woman I love.

IT is always telling lies. One lie is that IT can be fully gratified. Our proprium thinks that if IT gets what IT wants, IT will be gratified. But IT won't be gratified. We know that our love of the world, our love of power and money, will never be satisfied. We want not only all the money in the world, we want all the money in the universe. We don't want all the power in the world, we want all God's power as well. We know that, because the Writings teach it, and because, if we pay attention to our internal, we find that it is true. Before the Hunt brothers manipulated the stock market, they had two billion dollars. Were they satisfied? No, they wanted to get all the silver in the world, so they could have three billion dollars! J. Paul Getty did have three billion dollars. Did he say, "Hey, hold it, I think I have enough?" No, he wanted more. Well, that was not J. Paul Getty — that was J. Paul Getty's proprium, which happens to live in the same hell in which your proprium and my proprium live. The proprium will never be satisfied.

How do we wake up? Both Gurdjieff and Carlos Castaneda were concerned with waking people up to reality. They also came to the same conclusion: it is probably impossible. We can't wake people up. The only thing that will wake us up is the realization that a train is coming on the track. Then, we wake ourselves:

"Hey, buddy, a train's coming."

"Whoa!" And we wake up!

The train is coming, and it is our death. We don't know when it is going to arrive, but It is going to come, and when it comes, there will not be a second chance to wake up. A few people have had near-death experiences, but not many. Basically, when death comes, that is it! We may say, "Yeah, well, so what? So I die. I'm going to die eventually, anyway." However, if we have not spiritually awakened while in the natural world, we do not spiritually awaken after death. We stay the way we were in the natural world, spiritually asleep.

In *The Spiritual Diary*, Swedenborg gives several examples of the kind of spiritual sleep experienced by people in hell. In one instance, people are running around on a nice, grassy field, although when the field is seen in the light of heaven, there are a lot of snakes and unpleasant things around, but the people don't realize that, because they are in hell. Are they spiritually awake? No, they are in a fantasy, a dream. They are asleep. In another example, we see a person counting money. He thinks that he has all the money in the world. But, right beside him is someone else who is also counting money and who also thinks that he has all the money in the world! They are spiritually sound asleep and they don't care. Swedenborg quotes these spirits as saying, "We know that' it is total fantasy, but let us have our fantasies." They are asleep in a fantasy and they remain in a fantasy for eternity.

If we remain spiritually asleep, we choose not to participate in the Lord's work of creating, sustaining and caring for God's universe. When we choose spiritual sleep, we do not have a conscious relationship with the Lord. We do not allow God's love to come through us. We do not feel the pleasure the Lord gets as creator. Rather, we live in some hazy, dreamy sort of fantasy.

All negative emotions divide us one from another. As that mid-level manager who is spiritually asleep, my negative emotions will separate me for months from John Jones and from my boss — IT will separate me from them. If we act with consciousness, the Lord works through us to unite us. The Lord will unite us with our children, our friends, our spouses, our employees, our employers. The Lord wishes to see us joined, whereas the hells wish to divide us. The costs of identifying with negative emotions include divisiveness.

Our sources of knowledge consistently admonish us to awaken and become free of the prison we are in. Carlos Castaneda writes:

> There are some people who are very careful about the nature of their acts. Their happiness is to act with the full knowledge that they don't have time. There is a strange, consuming happiness in acting with the full knowledge that whatever one is doing may well be one's last act on earth.

Before knowledge has become a frightening affair, the man also realizes that death is the irreplaceable partner that must sit next to him. A man who follows the path becomes keenly aware of his death. Without the awareness of death, he would be only an ordinary man evolving in ordinary, mechanical life. A man has to be, first of all, and rightly, so keenly aware of his own death, but not to be concerned with his death, because to do so would force one to focus on oneself, and this would be debilitating. So the next thing for him to do is to be detached. The knowledge of his death will guide him and make him detached.

Nicoll, in *Commentaries*, says:

> In esoteric teaching, we are always told that we are in prison. All wrong emotions keep us in this prison.

Discipline is needed in regard to negative emotions. It must begin with self-observation. You must know and acknowledge when you are being negative. It is necessary to find and invent every method you can to prevent recurring events from making you negative.

In *Divine Love and Providence*, we find a parallel passage:

If man is in an infernal society, he can be led out of it only by the Lord, in accordance with the laws of Divine Providence, among which is this: That the man must see that he is there, he must wish to go out of it, and he must try to do this of himself. This he can do while he is in the world, but not after death, for he then remains forever in the society into which he has inserted himself while he is in the world. This is the reason why man must examine himself. He must recognize and acknowledge his sins, he must repent and then he must persevere even to the end of his life. (278 [6])

Through self-observation, we learn where we are presently in our spiritual life. Through self-observation, we understand the nature of our proprium and how much of our lives we are spending as servants identified with IT, making IT our own. The more we observe, the more we see that this is very serious business. If we live now in ITs negative states, we will continue after death to live in negative states in the spiritual world. We want to free our spirit from IT while we live in the natural world, because that is the purpose of our life in the natural world. We must begin by being awake to IT. We must see ITs nature. Only then can a new will be formed that will make possible our escape from ITs domination.

THE TASK:

To observe:

(1) A negative emotion, such as anger, depression or envy, and the gratification that the proprium was enjoying, or looking forward to, before it was interfered with;

(2) The costs, to our bodies, to our relationships, and to us spiritually, of identifying with that negative emotion.

3

KNOWLEDGE
AND BEING

The Work tells us that we must work along two lines, knowledge and being. The line of knowledge includes reading, studying, hearing sermons and encountering esoteric ideas. The line of being is entirely different. It comes from applying the Work to ourselves, which allows being to change. As we apply the Work to ourselves, we acquire a new understanding of what our knowledge is teaching. Within each of these lines, there is a progression toward the other. The Writings make clear that there is a difference between good from truth, and truth from good — just as there is a difference between experience from knowledge, and knowledge from experience.

If we study skiing while we are actually on a ski slope, using what we are learning, we will get a deeper understanding of what we have been studying. It will be experiential; it will become our experience. Understanding something emotionally is very different than just having knowledge of something from studying it. It is important to understand things emotionally. Perhaps we have had the experience of knowing something for many years as a result of religious instruction, but understanding it for the first time only by applying it to our life. That understanding is a shift in our level of being. Before applying what we knew, we never had a real understanding of it, even though we knew it.

Referring to the parable about sowing seeds, Nicoll equates the seed that fell on stony ground with knowledge that falls where there is no experience: because there is no application of the knowledge to experience, there is no place for the knowledge to take root. When the storms of temptation come, they will dry up the unapplied knowledge, which then won't be available to serve us. Likewise, the parable about building our house on rock instead of sand tells us that our unapplied intellectual knowledge has no foundation that can withstand an attack by very strong negative emotions from the hells. Our intellectual understanding will be washed away. Knowledge without experience will not sustain us through our struggles with temptation.

The tasks we are doing give us a taste of applying our knowledge, but they are but one opportunity to apply the Work, the Writings and other esoteric teaching. We must apply what we learn whenever we can. If we learn something and then make an effort to apply it, we will get a different understanding of it through our efforts.

Knowledge is only knowledge. Experience is a state of being. Suppose that we want to learn about strawberries. Someone who has never studied strawberries, but who eats them every morning, could tell us what color they are, how the fresh ones taste different than the old ones, and what their texture and taste are like. Someone who has never eaten a strawberry, but has studied strawberries, could describe their vitamin content, how long they take to grow, the best climate for them, their shape and density, and the amount of water they need. She could give us lots of information, even though she's never eaten a strawberry. A third person, who has not only studied strawberries, but eats them as well, could certainly tell us even more than the first two. But *none* of them can give us the *experience* of tasting a strawberry.

It is the same with being. No matter how much we study or how much we learn, no one can ever give us the experience of applying truth in our lives. I think we are protected in that way. No one can regenerate for us. We must do that for ourselves. But we can get knowledge from any source. Someone who has studied strawberries but has not eaten them nonetheless can teach a strawberry-eater very useful things. In this process, the strawberry-eater will also gain things that go beyond knowledge: a person applying doctrine to her life in fact may know more about the subject of instruction than the instructor himself knows. In *The Fourth Way*, P.D. Ouspensky writes:

> The mind must change before the rest of man can change. This is the same teaching as in the Gospel, where it is said that a man must first repent, which really means, in Greek, "change his mind." To change one's

mind means to think in a new way. These thoughts open up new parts of your mind that otherwise would remain unused. You will begin to understand emotionally, to see the truth of things emotionally, and at once you will see endless meaning and you will understand how the Work is inexhaustible. Seeing by long inner Work and then choosing the finer, you will eventually will and ultimately live the finer. You must separate the finer from the coarser. This begins personal Work and takes a long time.

The object of this Work is to make us conscious, in one's self and to ourselves, to what is going on in us and to the vast inner traffic of thoughts and feelings that lie within. Here in this inner world and in what we select or reject in it, lies the key to this Work. How can I prove to you that a strawberry tastes different than an apple? Not by any formatory arguments, I can assure you. You must taste and see for yourself. How can I prove to you that to begin to feel the many influences of this Work is different from being soaked in life? Of course I cannot. Now you must understand that this doctrine of "I's," or states, does not relieve you of all responsibility. Only a fool can imagine that. To reject states, or "I's," and select states, or "I's," is a very real thing.

It is necessary to realize that there is not a single useful negative emotion, not useful in any sense. Next, we must realize that we can struggle with them. They can be conquered and they can eventually be destroyed.

There is in us a triad of emotion, thought and action. An external event takes place, we get an impression and we react. The event gives rise to an emotion that forms itself into a thought that manifests in an action. We can think of an electric cord setting off dynamite. Push the plunger, a current runs through the cord and there is an explosion. It is as simple as that: plunger, current, explosion. There is a mechanical, direct path through the triad that takes no thought and no attention. If someone turns a corner and bumps into me, it takes no thought and no attention to say, "Hey, watch where you're going, you stupid idiot." It happens automatically.

We are not in control of the thoughts and emotions that come into us. What, then, can we do? We cannot do, but we must do what we can. Fortunately, the will and the understanding are divided. We are given the freedom to control that part of our thought process that is called rationality. We are given the ability to draw our rationality up and look down at events from what we have learned from doctrine, from what has been revealed to us about the nature of our proprium and feelings, and from the things that we have learned from the Work. This we can do if we wish. At the moment someone turns a corner and bumps into us and we feel a rush of emotion and hear the internal dialogue — at that moment, we can, with practice, draw our attention up into self-observation, into the rational. We can observe the event from the Work, as we have been doing in the tasks.

We can think of this effort and attention as a circuit breaker between the plunger and the coming explosion of negative expression. When a strong external event happens, we feel emotion and have negative internal dialogue, which remind us to do the Work. We attempt not to identify and to observe ourselves and what is going on as we draw up into the rational part of our mind. This breaks the circuit and prevents the explosion.

If we withdraw from the negative sooner, perhaps at the half-way point, we may say as much as, "Hey, watch where you're..." but then we turn passive. We have the negative thoughts, we have the feelings, but we desist, we do not act from them. We resist temptation. We are tempted to act mechanically, but we resist in light of what we know about the Work, about the nature of the proprium, about love of self and love of the world as opposed to love of the neighbor and love of the Lord. We can do this much and the Lord will do the rest.

We also have thoughts and feelings when there are no external events to which we attribute them. The nature of the thinking process that goes on in us when no notable external events are taking place is part of the focus of our current task. Swedenborg writes about this process in *Arcana Celestia:*

> The interior man perceives what is going on in the external man just as if someone were to tell him of that activity. (1701)

> In man, the spiritual world is conjoined with the natural

world, consequently the spiritual world flows into the
natural world in such a vivid manner that he can notice
it, provided that he pays attention. (6057)

In *Heaven and Hell*, he writes about our observation of the
process:

> If man's intentions are heavenward, his thought is deter-
> mined heavenward and with it his whole mind, which is
> thus in heaven, and from heaven he beholds the things
> of the world beneath him, like one looking down from
> the roof of a house. So the man who has the interiors of
> his mind open can see the evils and falsities that are with
> him, for these are below the spiritual mind. On the
> other hand, the man with whom the interiors have not
> been opened is unable to see his evils and falsities
> because he is not above them but is in them. (532)

And in *Apocalypse Revealed*, he notes that we cannot observe
without drawing up into our rational:

> Few men in the world know what their affections and
> thoughts are because being in them they thence do not
> reflect upon them. (536)

We can take the feeling of who we are out of the proprium and
put it into the observing part of us, into the observing "I" that is
the rational. That is possible for us to do. If we do our observing
during our quiet times, as well as during our active states, we learn
a lot about ourselves. Suppose that a boss tells a group of employees, "Take the day off, go into the city, or do whatever you want."
One employee might choose to go to a bar, while another might
choose a go-go dance. Some might go to a museum, or to a bookstore, or for a walk in the park. What these people choose to do
with their time when they are not pushed tells us a great deal about
them.

It is the same with the thoughts that we have when there is no
input from external events. Swedenborg tells us to observe our
thoughts in our quiet times in order to see where we are in the spiritual world. If we do so, we see what we are drawn to, what the
loves of our proprium are, what excites and delights IT. We find
out what IT likes to daydream about. When Pennsylvania's lottery
prize was forty-six million dollars, I had a lot of daydreams about

winning and about what a great guy I would be if I kept only thirty million for myself. I would be so charitable with the rest if only I kept that amount, or maybe thirty-five million — well, okay, maybe thirty-eight million. These are the kind of thoughts we are to watch. Often, we think such thoughts are good. What we want to do is observe them and see their real nature.

When it appears that we are merely daydreaming, we are establishing the pathways that we will use when there is a strong external event. Suppose that I am in the habit of just wandering about in the woods near my house, treading on wildflowers and knocking down little trees. I wander in the woods day in and day out, and eventually I establish certain paths. A day arrives when, while I am in the woods, I notice a fire truck coming and see that my house is on fire. I will definitely run through the pathways that I have already established — I will not, at that critical time, establish a new path. This situation is analogous to the pathways I establish in my proprium when I daydream about what I would do with my lottery winnings. Quiet time is not time that has no impact on us; we may be feeding the proprium, making it vigorous and strong. When we want to fight IT, we find that IT is very powerful because we have been feeding IT all the time, even when we are quiet. We may wish to put the proprium on a diet.

Maurice Nicoll writes about pictures. Consider my daydreamed "picture" of myself as a charitable person with forty-six million dollars. That picture has nothing to do with my reality. It certainly has nothing to do with the true nature of my proprium, which designed the picture in order to hide behind it. Similarly, if I think I am the kind of person who never gets mad, then I carry with me a picture that portrays me as someone who never gets mad. With that picture established, I am unlikely to notice when I am mad. The pictures we make during our quiet times influence us strongly.

We also tend to set the tone of our dominant mood during our quiet times. Of course, throughout each day, we have reactions. A guy bumps into our car, or someone compliments us, or someone tells us that we did a good job or a bad job, and we react emotionally. But between those events, we have a dominant mood, a way of approaching life. Some of us are sort of cynical, others are slightly depressed, some of us may be a little hyper. The thoughts that we have in our quiet times, and the emotions that are attached to them, establish the pathways of our dominant mood.

Observing the parts of the spiritual world that we tend to visit in our quiet times can show us what the proprium likes to do in ITs time off, as well as the source of our dominant mood. I notice that I am often cynical and irritable, especially when I read the newspaper. When I read the paper, I tend to read articles, for example, about judges being paid off. No wonder I am cynical! I visit cynical places in the spiritual world. Thus I am feeding my proprium "cynical food," making IT ever more cynical and irritable.

We have an inherited way of seeing things that is like having several pairs of colored eyeglasses. We are always looking at the world through one or another of those pairs of glasses. When we're in a blue mood, we think the world really is blue. When we are looking through our red glasses, we think that the world is red. Even when we pull ourselves up by means of our rationality, we still do not see the world objectively. What we see objectively is ourselves looking at the world subjectively — we may even hear ourselves saying, "Gee, I'm wearing red glasses, and this proprium of mine really thinks the world is red. That's really amazing!" We tend to polish the eyeglasses that we like best, and to keep them, and the moods that they represent, closest to us. Our favored glasses are the ones we tend to put on in our quiet times. We will observe these moods as part of our task.

The difference between objective and subjective consciousness is hard to envision. I do know that if I have been identified, and then I am able to stop being identified, the world looks very different: I am seeing objectively myself experiencing the world subjectively. I'm sure that objective consciousness is even clearer than that. We want to see the causes of things. After near-death experiences, people have said, "I suddenly saw the purpose in everything. I really saw what it is all about. It makes sense; it is logical." There is a state of consciousness in which everything makes sense and in which there is nothing that does not make sense. I have only heard about that state, but I believe that it exists, and I think that objective consciousness is something like that. The celestial angels are unique. They are created in a form different from any other. The Lord flows through them, and they are deeply conscious of the Lord's presence, but they are also exquisitely conscious of their individuality.

The task is to observe our thoughts during quiet times. We will observe our thoughts, and then observe the emotion that results from those thoughts. Or, we may observe an emotion first, and then observe the thoughts that accompany that emotion. It can go either way. Once we have observed our thoughts and emotions, regardless of the order in which they come, we will try to stop the thoughts and observe the impact of that on the emotions.

We will observe the mood that we would set for ourselves if we continued with our thoughts. For instance, if I am thinking about what I'm going to do tomorrow, anxiety may attack me. If I continue with those thoughts, I will establish a mood of anxiety during that time, and that is what I will be: I will be anxiety for that time. Anxiety is what those thoughts will produce in me. But if I stop the thoughts, I will experience an entirely different state. Therefore, when we are aware of an emotion, we will step back, observe, and ask, "What thought am I having?" Or, if we are aware of a thought, we will observe it, and ask, "What emotion am I having?" Then, we will stop the thought and observe what happens to the emotion.

THE TASK:

During our quiet times:

(1) To observe our thoughts and emotions;

(2) After observing them, to stop our thoughts and observe the impact on our emotions.

4

REMEMBERING OURSELVES

Suppose that we are talking with a child. In our cupboard, there are both a Tiffany crystal glass and an old, scratched, rough beer mug that was made from a beer bottle. We put these next to one another on the counter and ask the child, "Which is the good glass and which is the bad glass?" The child might say, "The pretty one is the good glass."

We go to the refrigerator, get some cola and pour it into the beer mug. We go to the stove, get some black coffee and pour it into the crystal. Then we ask the child again, "Which is the good glass and which is the bad one?" The child might say, "Oh, now the good glass is over here," pointing to the one with the cola in it.

However, we might get a different answer if, after cleaning both glasses, we poured coffee into the mug and cola into the crystal and then asked someone who really liked coffee which was the good glass.

The content is not the glass. The mug and the crystal glass can contain different things. As long as we can wash them out, the crystal may appear to be the better glass, because even if it has poison in it, it is a fine glass. But, suppose that we were giving a beer party at which we would be serving foreign beers, and that our beer mug happened to be made from a foreign beer bottle, and that at our party, we were going to have that kind of beer on tap — then, that beer mug would be a pretty good glass for our party.

Now, however, let's suppose that once we fill one glass with coffee and the other with cola, from that day on, magically, they will yield only what they have been filled with. We will have to look at those glasses differently, because no matter how much we drink from the one with coffee in it, it is always going to give out coffee; it is never going to give anything else. We now have to evaluate them differently.

When we are in the other world after death, that which is in us will continue to flow from us, as from a vessel. But prior to death, we have the opportunity to choose what comes into our vessel and what flows out of it. We are not the cola. We are not the coffee. We are the vessel. We are aware of thoughts and feelings as they actually enter us. We choose those things that we wish to have in our vessel, and those things that we wish to flow from our vessel. We gain a sense of where our value to the Lord lies. The Lord created us as vessels. Our heredity gives us certain contents, but our value is in our *vesselness*, in our ability to receive, rather than in what we are filled with at this moment. What we are filled with at this moment is what we don't want to identify with. We read in Nicoll's Commentaries

> It is a very marvelous thing to experience a moment of not being identified. When you are in such a state, you seem to live in a quiet and central place in yourself, although you are aware that on all sides things are flowing in and trying to advance on you. Once more, I will say to you that when you are trying to observe yourself, you must not put the feeling of who you are into the feeling of what you observe — you must put it into the observing part of yourself.

Understanding the relationship between the Work and the Writings helps us to understand truths and to live them. But we may ask, why don't we just stay within the Gurdjieff/Nicoll system, since we may best understand its application to our lives? For myself, I believe that the Writings are revealed by God. I have no question but that they are revelation. Perhaps Gurdjieff drew from an ancient revelation, but I don't know that — we don't know his source. I use the Writings as a standard against which to measure any system, and the Work and the Writings really do complement each other. Thus, as we come across different terms and concepts in Gurdjieff, Ouspensky and Nicoll, I try to compare them with the Writings.

The Work refers a good deal to three levels of influence — A, B, and C-influences. A-influences are basically worldly knowledge, or information. If we read newspapers, we get a lot of A-influences. B-influences involve psychology, philosophy and religion.

These are called derived doctrines, which are concepts arrived at from weighing what doctrines indicate or mean. These concepts have to do with changing and bettering who we are in terms of our spiritual life, rather than our natural life. C-influences comprise revelation that is conscious in its origin, and they are the only influences that actually bring about transformation, or regeneration. B-influences can bring us to a state in which we recognize and receive C-influences, but only C-influences can save us.

In church, a minister reads from revelation, or C-influences. But a minister also gives a sermon, interpreting in derived doctrine what she understands revelation to say. That sermon is a B-influence. However, we must go to revelation ourselves and not depend upon B-influences, because no one else can give us C-influences. For instance, when a minister is reading from revelation, our actual reception of C-influences depends upon our own state, upon where we are spiritually. It is very doubtful that a person in church who is thinking about the cocktail party that he is going to have afterwards — are there enough snacks? is there enough to drink? — is receiving C-influences.

B-influences are like the light in winter. That light can be very bright and very beautiful on a gorgeous winter day. The ice can be sparkling. If I find a sunny place, it might even feel warm enough to take my jacket off. But with so little heat, that winter light cannot start a germination process. It cannot transform a cold, sleeping world into springtime. However, when the spring heat does arrive, or when the world turns toward the heat and comes closer to its source, something brand new takes place. When affection for good enters, the new will is born, which is delight in doing good. There is a real experience of change in ourselves and our relationships. When spiritual germination takes place, a change occurs and a whole new relationship is born.

To enter the stream of Providence with a real change of will, we must trust in the Lord and see the Lord in all things at the time that those things are actually taking place. To trust that the Lord is overseeing the very situation that we are in and to see the Lord's laws in everything, consciously and actively looking for those laws, is to see our situation from doctrine, or the Lord's point of view. That allows us to enter the stream of Providence, where transformation, or regeneration, can take place. Regeneration can't take place if we are asleep, but if we are looking at things from doctrine, the truth can germinate in us.

The Work speaks often of our "magnetic center," which is an inner longing for esoteric truth. I believe that it is the love of knowing, which is a love that we are born with. It is a love that precedes the love of truth for truth's sake, which is called rationality. Magnetic center is what motivates us to page through the Work or the Writings, or to go to a bookstore looking for esoteric knowledge. We have a desire to know. If magnetic center brings together enough of the "I's" of our Work, it can help produce in us something that resists our personality and our proprium.

The Work also frequently refers to "remembering ourselves." That involves remembering our aim, our goal in life, and having the awareness that "I am," in the sense of being a vessel. The awareness that the Lord is present is very important. Gurdjieff was fond of saying that we should remember ourselves at least once a day, but that if we could not remember ourselves once a day, then we should remember ourselves three times a day. I think that he was indicating how much repetition would help to establish the habit. Ouspensky, in *The Fourth Way*, writes about self-remembering:

> You have to begin by studying what self-remembering means intellectually, but in actual fact it is not intellectual, because it is a moment of will. It is necessary to remember yourself, not only in a quiet moment when nothing is happening, but when you know that you are doing something wrong and then not do it. For instance, when you are identified, you must be able to feel it and then stop it, and at the same time remember yourself.

As does Nicoll, in *Commentaries*

> You do not even realize that you are playing the typical role that millions of others have played and are playing, and that you will not get free from it unless you wake up and see that you are not usually remembering yourself.

> Do you remember how the Work is defined in Hebrews? It is called logos, or the Word: the Word of God is living and active and sharper than any two-edged sword, and piercing, even to dividing the soul and spirit of both

joints and marrow, and quick to discern the thoughts
and the feelings of the heart.

Two additional very powerful tools that we have are awareness and attention. We may think that we have only a certain
amount of attention or a certain level of awareness, but we can
increase our awareness and attention. Gurdjieff says that awareness is a substance and that the more we use it, the more is created.
We can be aware that we love our spouse or our friend, but the
level of our awareness of that love can change from hour to hour.
Momentarily, we will do a visualization involving changing the
level of our awareness.

Attention is the same way. We can increase it or decrease it. A
basketball referee has an attention to the game that is different
than the crowd's. People in the crowd are eating hot dogs and
drinking beer and sort of watching the game while also talking to
their friends. But when the referee calls a foul on their team, they
jump up and yell, "You fool! Don't you have eyes? Can't you see
what's going on?" They accuse the referee of having no attention
when they aren't paying any attention themselves. However, the
fans of the other team don't jump up and yell, because they aren't
aware and are totally identified. Thus, there are different degrees
of attention.

We can use our right brains to do a visualization that applies
these ideas. Let's take a few deep breaths and let ourselves relax,
close our eyes and just listen and be aware. We may be aware, for
instance, of sitting on a couch, or on a chair. We can be aware of
our body, and we can even allow ourselves, and allow our awareness to allow us, to relax a little more. We can be aware of the
muscles in our arms and we can relax them. We can be aware of
our breathing and that we are where we are, relaxing more and
more.

The Work tells us that to remember ourselves is to be aware
that we are where we are. A moment ago, we may have been
thinking about the past or about the future. We may have been
experiencing internal dialogue. But if we will just be aware that we
are where we are now, in this room, in this house, in this town, and
increase that awareness, right now, we will become aware of being
a small part of the universe. Right here, in this place, we can be
aware that we are a very little dot in a vast universe. We really are
right here, and there really is a universe, and we really are just a lit-

tle spot, right here.

We may also be aware of people around us, and that these people have names, but that they are not their names. We may be aware, perhaps, of what they look like, but each of these people has thoughts and feelings and experiences that we know nothing about. We can be aware that we know only a little about these people. Each of them has an attachment to the spiritual world. They have spirits around them, and each is a manifestation of thousands and millions of things going on, connecting them and us and everything, all the way to the Lord.

We can also be aware that there is no time and there is no space. We are in an unfathomable, indescribable universe right now. That awareness is ours and can increase. We can learn to use that awareness and to increase it at any time.

We also have attention, and we can put that attention on our hand. We can put enough attention on our hand that we can actually feel a certain spot there. Our hand was there before, but now we are more aware of it, directing our attention to it. In the future, when we have a strong negative emotion, we can put our attention on our hand and quiet our mind and just experience that emotion until it, too, becomes quiet. And, over time, by controlling our attention, relaxing our body and, at the same time, stopping our internal dialogue, we can gain control of our emotions, being aware that we are not those emotions, but are only vessels, and that when emotions flow in, we do have the control to stop all thought, to totally relax our body and to just be with those emotions until we experience change. We can let in the thought that all states do change. We can invite higher influences into our consciousness.

We can have an awareness of being where we are now, an awareness of our body, of our ability to relax and our ability to stop thought. We can increase our awareness and increase our attention. We can use them for the Work at any time. We become aware of being where we are now, returning slowly and pleasantly, finding ourselves alert and refreshed from a little time out. We feel the chair beneath us and we picture the room that we are in, and, when we are ready, we open our eyes and are really here.

The heart and the lungs support each other in carrying out their tasks in the body: the heart muscle uses a great deal of oxygen that the lungs provide, and the lungs use a great deal of blood that the heart provides. Good and truth support each other, however they can, wherever they are. In the same sense, we must bring something good to any situation out of which we hope to get something, because what we get out of a situation usually depends upon what we bring to it. Bringing our awareness and our attention to a situation is important.

Suppose that we plan to hear a speaker whom we really like. We are excited about it, looking forward to it, and when we are there, we really pay attention and we hear a good talk. Then, suppose that we go to hear another speaker, but someone comes up to us beforehand and whispers, "I'm not very interested — this speaker doesn't give the kind of lectures I want to hear." We may lose our interest, only half-listen, and go away disappointed. Now, if the two speakers happened to switch their talks, we would probably still have the same experience, even though they each gave the other's talk. And why is that? It is because what we get out of something depends upon what we bring to it, not upon the event itself. The appearance is that the cause of a good talk is in the speaker, but that is only an appearance. The real truth is that the value we get out of it depends upon what we bring to it.

The Writings tell us of influx and that the value we get from something depends upon the "extension of our mind into the internal world." If we are thinking at a natural, corporeal level, the extension of our mind into the spiritual world is like shining a flashlight in a deep fog. But if we raise ourselves up into our rational, the extension of our mind into the spiritual world is like a light on a clear night. There are more spirits in touch with our spirit, which is in the spiritual world. Because of the extension, we get much more out of what we are listening to. It is because of what we bring to it, not just what is given to us.

Think of Newton, sitting in an orchard when an apple fell on his head. Now, many people sat in orchards and many people saw apples fall — why do we remember the name Newton? What was different? It was what Newton brought to that event, not the apple falling, that was special. We might say that it was what Newton knew, but the truth is that often the value is in what we don't know. For instance, most people once knew that the world was flat, but there was one fellow who didn't know that, which led to the discovery that the world is round.

Einstein was known for being a genius, and we might say that he was a genius because of all he knew, but to some degree he was a genius because of what he didn't know. For example, it was known that if a person next to us walked toward the horizon, it appeared that they got smaller. But Einstein said, "The person is getting smaller. It's obvious. You can see it." And we responded, "Oh, no, no. If we measure her with a ruler here, she's 5'6" tall, and if we follow her to the horizon and measure her there, even though she looks only this big now, she'll still be 5'6" tall — won't she?" Einstein replied, "No. Your ruler is getting smaller, too. I can see it."

When we give up what we *think* we know, we get to learn things that we did not know. If we listen to someone with the idea that what we believe will be confirmed, then what we get is what we already know. If we listen with the idea that someone is wrong when we disagree, then we get to confirm what we already know, but we don't get to know something brand new. The level at which we listen is very important. Quieting the external mind and allowing ourselves to be open, so that the extension of our mind goes further into the spiritual world, is important. Being open to new ideas, to new thoughts and feelings, is a new experience called remembering ourselves. In *The Fourth Way*, Ouspensky puts it like this:

> All I can say is that what you do today makes tomorrow. So tomorrow depends on what you do today. You can change the future right now. That is what must be understood.

THE TASK:

(1) To remember ourselves once a day, even if we are not sure what that is;

(2) To repeat the visualization, if we wish.

5

CHOOSING NEVER TO
EXPRESS A NEGATIVE

When we are in church, we are likely to be concentrating on B and C-influences, trying to hear revelation from a higher part of our mind. One way to do that is stop internal dialogue. If we stop internal dialogue, we quietly listen, rather than reacting to what is said with, "Yes, but..."

When a minister speaks from derived doctrine, some of the things said may be true and some may not be true. I think of it as similar to eating a meal: if the meal is generally healthy, we can take it in and enjoy it. We can allow our digestive system to sort out what is healthy and what is not, what is useful and what can be done away with. When we go to church, we can quiet our mind and let our internal sort what is useful from what is not. Our mind is open in a different way when we are not trying to judge or evaluate what we hear on a formatory level, but rather are just letting new ideas come in. Stopping our internal dialogue thus is one way of approaching situations that may contain B and C-influences.

In the preceding chapter, we mentioned that the Writings and the Work can be parallel. In *Apocalypse Explained*, Swedenborg seems to echo what we have just discussed about receiving B and C-influences:

> For man is in his proprium when he is solely in his external natural man, but is elevated from his proprium when he is in his internal spiritual man. That he has been elevated from his proprium is not felt by the man except from the fact that at that time he does not think evils and that he is averse to thinking them and that he is delighted with truths and with goods. Nevertheless,

man, if he progresses further into the state, perceives the influx with some thought, but still he is not withheld from thinking and willing as if this were from himself. (945)

And in *Spiritual Diary*, he writes:

If man would attend to reflection he would find more secrets in the doctrine of reflection than in any other. What reflection performs may be evident when one considers that he perceives no sense in any part of his body unless he reflects on that part. (733)

Man learns from the Word what is good and true in order that he may reflect on these in himself, which reflection is given him at certain times, especially in times of trouble. Therefore to know the truth is of the greatest moment for without knowledge there can be no reflection and thus no reformation. (737)

We can compare these excerpts with Nicoll, in *Commentaries*

Have you yet begun to separate from yourself or from your machine? You chatter away, you criticize all day as if you knew. You do not yet even notice that you do not know, that you really have not yet the faintest idea that you are talking nonsense and lying all day. Because there is no self-noticing, there is no inner sincerity.

Perhaps some of us had a negative reaction to Nicoll. That reaction is from our proprium. If we paraphrase the excerpt, we may be able to separate from our reaction:

Have you yet begun to separate yourself from your proprium? IT chatters away and IT criticizes all day as if IT knew. IT does not notice that IT does not know, that IT really has not the faintest idea of what IT is talking about. IT talks nonsense and IT lies all day.

We are not our proprium, but our proprium really does do all the things Nicoll describes.

The Work tells us, "Never express a negative." There are three different states in which the nonexpression of negatives can occur: a state of suppression, a state of obedience, or a state of choice.

With suppression, there is denial. Consider someone who carries a picture of himself as a very calm person. Everyone else may hear the anger in his voice and see by his cheek muscles that he is angry, but his picture of himself leads him to believe that he is not angry. Therefore, he is in denial. Denial prevents him from working on his anger because he is not conscious that he *is* angry.

I believe that denial is represented in the Bible by the Hebrew slaves. The slaves in Egypt have not realized that they are the chosen people. They are slaves despite being created to be something else. They are not yet conscious of the reality of their situation because it seems so natural for them to be slaves. They are in a state of suppression.

All of us are in a state of slavery. We may carry pictures portraying us as good people because we do not express anger in our external behavior. But they are only pictures, if our internal is anger and we do not treat others internally as we treat them externally. Those "I's" in us are asleep. They are in denial.

A state of obedience in the nonexpression of negatives may be described as a person who is aware of her anger, but does not express it because she believes that the Lord asks her not to. She is acting from truth and her behavior is from obedience, that is, from faith, since it is from knowledge. In refusing to act against that knowledge, she is a good and faithful servant. We can think of her as analogous to a house. Evil spirits have slipped in the back door and sneaked through the basement windows. The Lord has asked her to keep them from hurting her neighbors, so she doesn't let them out, *but they are in the house.* Protecting others from the hells within us is obedience.

We aim to reach a state in which we *choose* not to express negative emotions, in which we see in their evil nature the reason not to express them. The state of choice comes from understanding that we are the vessel rather than the emotion that fills it. We choose not to permit evil spirits into our house.

This form of the nonexpression of negatives differs sharply from the state of obedience. As we do the Work, we find that sometimes the hells knock at our door, masquerading as the bishop come to tea. But we've been had a few times already, and we've acquired a feel for the hells, an ability to smell them, so we don't let them slip in. We separate from the negative and do not identify with it. Our house becomes clean and empty and ready for something else. We make a choice.

We make that choice when we understand, affectionally and emotionally, that we do not want evil spirits in our house because they do damage to us, to those we love, and to the community. That choice allows us to be friends with the Lord, rather than only obedient servants. That choice is the truest nonexpression of negatives.

It is important to remember that we are not adding to ourselves, we are taking away, or simplifying. We aim for a state that is childlike in its willingness to let the Lord work through us. We choose to clean our house and make it empty of devils in preparation for the entry of the Lord. We are using a lot of words to talk about that, and acquiring a lot of left-brain data, but it really has an intuitive, right-brain aspect, which we can appreciate through a visualization:

So let us now just relax. Let us close our eyes and get physically comfortable. Let us be aware of our body and the rhythm of our breathing. There is now no need for left-brain thinking, just the awareness of our body relaxing, of its position, of our hands or perhaps of our feet. Let us be aware that we have a body, but we are not that body, which someday we will leave for an experience that is more alive, more vivid, more real. We feel sensations, but we are not those sensations. We have thoughts, but we are not our thoughts. We have feelings, but we are not our feelings. We are a vessel that receives life and has experiences, internal and external.

In our experience we have many memories, including memories of our childhood. We remember being a little child on a vacation near water, and we recall the sounds of the water breaking on the shore and lapping against a dock and a boat. We recall the warmth of the sun, the warmth of a rock as we lay against it in our bathing suit, the smell of the water turning to steam on the heat of the rock, the sounds of the birds overhead.

We remember also being a child and going to the refrigerator for our favorite drink. We remember, as we drank, wanting the taste of that drink to stay with us forever, making the taste of that drink a part of who we are. We remember, too, a time when we tasted something that we did not like at all, and we remember wanting it not to be a part of us, and spitting it out to get rid of it.

We remember our house in the springtime, opening the windows and doors to let in the warm breezes to take away the cold of winter, and we recall wanting to bring inside as much of the outdoors as possible, the warmth and the sounds and the smells and the colors, to fill our house with springtime.

We remember also the clouds covering the sun and recall feeling a chill and hearing distant thunder and feeling falling rain and closing the doors and windows of our house, turning lights on and putting some wood on the fire to make it safe and warm inside, close to the light and the heat.

We remember learning as a child that we could let certain things in and also keep certain things out. Things like springtime we welcomed and breathed in deeply, wanting to make them a part of who we are, feeling the warmth of the sun on our face. Things like wintertime we didn't like and shut out, closing our doors and windows against the chill, making inside warm and safe. We remember that we learned these things as a child from our experience, and that with this knowledge from our experience, we made choices to open ourselves to certain things, and also to turn away from other things that we did not let in.

As we return from our visualization, we can bring with us both our realization that we are a vessel that receives life and our memories of our experiences with the importance of choosing to open ourselves to certain things.

The Work uses the concept of recurrence, that is, that the same spiritual problems will recur in our lives if we continue to act mechanically from our proprium. A bitter young person becomes a bitter old person. Someone contemptuous of people with money will be contemptuous of people without money if she eventually becomes wealthy. The particular object of her contempt will change, but she will meet her contempt every day of her life unless she does the Work. Her contempt will recur.

If we see that the source of our problems is within us, and if we separate from IT and do not identify with IT and do not express ITs negatives, the world we perceive will change and we will not meet those problems again. Of course, we then will meet different problems that will require us to apply the Work, but the old problems will not recur.

When we meditate on the Word of God, we are doing what the Work calls "long thinking." Swedenborg mentions what we can recognize as aspects of long thinking in *Divine Love and Wisdom*

> Appearances are the first thing out of which the human
> mind forms its understanding and the mind can shake
> these appearances off only by the death of the causes,

> and if the causes lie deeply hidden, the mind can explore
> only by keeping the understanding for a long time in
> spiritual life, and this it cannot do because of natural
> life, which continually tries to withdraw it. (40)

It takes effort and attention to keep our thinking in spiritual life, that is, thinking from the rational. Most simply, long thinking is thinking about the state we are in rather than *from* the state we are in. Thinking from a negative state produces only lies, but it is possible for us to think about IT from the rational, from what we understand from doctrine and the Word and Revelation, our B and C-influences. When we do this, we are using the Work as a neutralizing force.

In every endeavor, there is an active force and a resistant force. Any effort we make will meet resistance at some point. We can picture these forces as a triangle. Active force can be described as the way we desire our life to go. For example, we start a diet and vow to stay on it, or we resolve that we will exercise every day.

The resistant force is the cake that tempts us to abandon our diet, or the cold weather that discourages us from jogging. The resistant force is life proceeding against our desires. When we encounter the resistant force, we can be angry at life and fight with it, or we can look for a neutralizing force.

The Work is the neutralizing force. When we use the neutralizing force, we recognize that our life is perfect, in that it provides us with exactly those problems on which we need to work. It is no mistake that I feel impatient while waiting for my train, or that another commuter is bored, while a third is anxiously planning her day. It is the same late train for all of us. And it provides each of us with the perfect opportunity to work on those things that are problems for us. This is because our experience of life comes from where our spirit is in the spiritual world, or, as the Work says, from our level of being. The encounter between our will and the resistant force produces in us the very state on which we need to work, and simultaneously provides us the opportunity to do so. If we do the Work, the state will not recur. If we do not do the Work, we will get another opportunity to do so five minutes from now, or tomorrow, or next week, for the rest of our life.

When we interpose the neutralizing force of the Work between the active and resistant forces, we transform our relationship to the world. Our negative states become an alarm clock. Every time we experience a negative state, the alarm clock goes off. Time to work! What do we work on? Our own state, as it is right here, right now. We work on that. Now is the time to work. Work is the neutralizing force. The Work enables us to transform B-influences into C-influences, to turn knowledge into understanding.

A person learning to ski has been told that he must shift his weight to the downhill ski when on the slope. He has learned that, memorized it — he has that knowledge. Where is he going to experience revelation about shifting his weight? On the slope. When he starts a turn, he will experience fear of shifting his weight to the downhill ski, that is, he will encounter the resistant force. If he overcomes that fear and shifts his weight, he will experience revelation and will no longer have merely knowledge, but understanding, and that understanding will become a part of who he is.

In terms of the doctrine of the Writings, the skier knows the truth that he must shift his weight. When he actually does it, although he really doesn't understand it and doesn't want to do it and is therefore afraid, his behavior is good from truth. And at the moment of that good, the skier has a revelation, which is truth from good. It is living truth. The difference between good from truth, and truth from good, is as between the winter light and the summer sun.

When the alarm clock of a negative state goes off and we are conscious of the Work as the neutralizing force, we recognize the perfect opportunity to work. We open to ourselves the possibility of revelation. The oscillation of good from truth, truth from good, good from truth, continues as long as we search for causes and use the truth we gain.

Real truth is a way of living, an experience, not merely something we think about. The menu is not the meal. There is a crucial difference between reading the menu and eating the meal. The menu describes the food, but our experience of eating the food is entirely different. Eating the meal involves a shift from knowledge of it to understanding it.

The task is to determine through self-observation how we remember to be negative. We have not discussed this before, but it is easy to give an example. One night recently, my train was running twenty minutes late. I knew that my wife had cooked dinner and expected me to take it out of the oven at a certain time. And I knew that I would probably not be home by then. I also knew that

I had to prepare a class I was giving later that evening. So I was negative. As I rode, I wondered, "How am I remembering that I'm late? How am I remembering that when I get home, the dinner will be burned? How am I reminding myself that there is a class tonight for which I may not have time to prepare?"

I stopped thought. When I did, I found that I was just riding a train. I wasn't sure if I was riding into or out of town, going to or coming from work. Frankly, the train could have been in Arizona for all I knew. Thus I became aware that I have to expend effort in order to maintain a negative attitude. I realized that it takes a certain amount of effort to hold in my awareness the things I use to create my negative attitudes. That night, I had to keep *reminding* myself that the train was late, that supper would burn (which it didn't), and that I might not have time to prepare class (which I did).

We spend a lot of our energy making sure we continue in negative states. The hells in us want to reside in negative states for as long as possible. Thus the hells keep reminding us of all the reasons we should give housespace to evil spirits. Our task is to observe that process, to observe and ask ourselves, "When I am in a negative state, how do I remember to be negative?"

THE TASK:

To determine through self-observation how we remember to maintain a negative state.

6

LETTING GO OF
IDENTIFICATION

In *Psychological Commentaries*, Nicoll suggests that each of us has a "chief feature." He also suggests that it is useless for us to be told about our chief feature because we won't believe it. However, Nicoll's "chief feature" is comparable to Swedenborg's "ruling love," and it is useful for us to know that we have a ruling love and that all our proprial loves are somehow attached to that ruling love. If, in cutting the roots of a briar plant while gardening, we find the tap root, we have discovered the chief feature of that plant. Likewise, through self-observation we learn that the different forms of our negative emotions tend toward one central ruling love, or chief feature. If our chief feature is love of dominion, we find irritation, impatience, anger and frustration nourishing that love of dominion like the roots of a briar plant. Here is Nicoll on chief feature:

> Since chief feature is the axle around which everything else turns, it is clear that if one wishes to really change, the central axle must eventually be taken out.
>
> [The ability] to see chief feature depends on one's power to endure it. We forget how sensitive we are to the slightest discouragement and criticism. In no case can anyone be told his or her chief feature because no one would believe it and then no one could stand it. The only way that you can endure it is by having something else that you can hold onto. You can then endure a certain amount of devaluation of yourself. In other words, you may be able to endure catching a glimpse from time

to time of your level of being.

> Full self-remembering is a state of consciousness in which the personality and all its pretense almost cease to exist and you are, so to speak, nobody, and yet the fullness of this state, which is really bliss, makes you, for the first time, *somebody.*

There are many spokes, but there is only one hub, as Swedenborg describes in *Arcana Celestia*:

> Ruling love induces a form on the will of every man. This love is in the middle and ordinates everything around itself, placing nearest itself the things which are in most agreement, and the rest in order according to their agreement. The ruling or reigning love, that is, the love of the thing which one has for an end, is what makes a man. This love has subordinated to it many particular and singular loves which are derivations and appear under another aspect, but still the ruling love is in each of them and directs them, and through them, as through a mediate end, regards and pursues its own end, which is the primary and ultimate end of all, both directly and indirectly. (6690)

The Writings also tell us of the need to discover our end in view in order to discover the purpose of what we are doing. Through self-observation, we can differentiate between our negative and our positive behavior. If we are behaving charitably, but wish to discover whether we are coming from a negative emotion, we look at the end in view: is the aim, or end, of our behavior the love of reputation, or is it real concern for the neighbor? When we find that answer, we know whether to apply the Work or simply let the charity flow through us.

We experience various degrees of identification with negative states, reflecting the distance of our observing "I" from the proprium. We may be angry and, in total denial, not know that we are angry. We may know that we are angry, but be totally identified. We may see that we are angry and separate a bit from our anger. Or, even better, we may see that IT is angry and that we need not be. If we can see that IT is angry, but simultaneously can feel peace, quietness, or even joy (feelings distinct from the anger that IT is feeling), we are much further along the road away from identification than is usual when we have just begun the Work.

Our awareness of our identification varies in relation to our different temptations and different states. Nicoll says that we are always identified and, because of that, don't even notice it, in the same way that we do not notice our body temperature because it is so constant. If our temperature goes up, however, we notice: "Oh, yes, I do have body heat — now it's a hundred and four." Our normal temperature is pretty warm, but we are unaware of it. Likewise, when our identification becomes very strong, we notice it and realize that we are identified all the time with states, usually negative.

For instance, I went to a high-school wrestling tournament. I bought a Coke and began to watch one of the many matches. As between those two wrestlers, I could not have cared less who won the match. However, as I watched them, I gradually did develop a preference for one of them: I rather liked the way he moved. I was becoming more identified with him than with his opponent. I felt happy when he was successful and a little upset when he was not. I moved closer to the mat and noticed that the wrestler I preferred was from my local high school. I became more identified with him. When I moved even closer, I saw that the wrestler I favored was a boy I knew, and I became even more identified with him.

On another occasion, I was looking for my team's fans at a football game. Where were they sitting? Where was the red and white? I could find no red and white, and my mind started racing: where am I? *who* am I? I was looking for my identity. When the teams came onto the field, both were dressed in white and had white helmets on. I didn't know *which* to identify with. I was in a state of confusion, because I might have found myself actually cheering for the opposition.

Our proprium looks for identities to attach ITSELF to in order to give meaning to our life. We search for identity to fill our emptiness. In occupations such as mine, people carry identification cards. I can show you my card as evidence of my identity — I am a Federal Probation Officer; it says so right on my card. Kids are searching for identity when they ask, "May I be your friend?" or, "Can I be on your team?" When others push us around, our proprium reaches for those things with which it is identified, and we respond, "Do you know who you are talking to?" and, "My father is so-and-so," or, "I belong to such-and-such." These are all instances of our proprium being identified.

At the football game, if I had stopped searching for my team, I would not have been so identified. Then I could have seen the game more objectively, and enjoyed the good plays regardless of which team made them. We want to develop the objectivity that comes when we separate from our proprium.

As a result of the Work, we stop identifying with the things that once gave us our self-importance. We no longer identify with our team losing, or our favorite politician winning, or any other specific thing or event. Instead, we work on ourselves. However, there is in this process a period during which we have given up our old identities, but yet don't have anything new in place. Gurdjieff called that state "being between stools." For instance, after they left Egypt, the children of Israel had feelings of discontent, and grumbled, "At least, back in Egypt, they gave us food." They missed their old state because they were not yet in the Land of Canaan, the new state of milk and honey.

When we are between stools, the hells attack us differently. They attack the Work, the journey itself. The hells no longer tell us, "You don't have to leave Egypt, you are okay." Rather, they say, "I'm sick of working. When are my habits, my same old attitudes, going to change?" We must approach such negative states toward the Work as we approach any negative state. We observe the internal dialogue, observe our emotional response to it, and do not identify with it. We work on such states as we work on other negative states. We continue to work.

Being between stools is actually an encouraging sign, for it means that we are no longer in Egypt. But we do not get our old gratifications. Out in the desert between Egypt and the Promised Land, we do not get the food that we were used to in Egypt. Manna tastes entirely different, even though it is much finer than anything we got in Egypt, and it lacks the intensity of the gratifications we experienced in Egypt. We must learn to appreciate a subtler gratification than our old delights gave us.

In the Work, the sequence of things is an important consideration, just as it is in building a house. I might learn the many things I need to know to build a house by studying electrical wiring and carpentry and plumbing, but still I might not understand the importance of sequence in building. I might finish pouring the concrete for the foundation before I discovered that I had not provided for the utility lines to come into the basement. Or, I might finish the drywalling, only to find that I had not put in the electrical outlets. Thus would I learn the importance of sequence.

In the following excerpts from Swedenborg's *Heaven and Hell*, we can see the implication of sequence by noticing what, of necessity, must be in place before a further stage may be reached. Sometimes it is very obvious; sometimes it is not:

> It is not so hard to lead a heaven-bound life as people think it is, because it is simply a matter of when something gets in the way that the person knows is dishonest and unfair, even something his spirit moves toward, of thinking he should not do it because it is against the Divine precepts. If a person gets used to doing this and by getting used to it gains a certain disposition to do so, then little by little he is bound to heaven. As this takes place the higher reaches of his mind are opened and as they are opened, he sees things that are dishonest and unfair and as he sees them, these can be broken apart. For no evil can be broken apart until it has been seen. This is a condition a person can enter because of his freedom, for who cannot think this way because of his freedom? And once this is begun the Lord works out all good things for him and arranges things so that he not only sees evil elements but dislikes them and eventually turns away from them. (533)

> If people only believed the way things really are — that everything good is from the Lord and everything evil from hell — then they would not make anything good in themselves a matter of merit, nor would anything evil be charged to them. For in that case they would focus on the Lord in everything good that they thought and did, and everything evil that flowed in they would throw back into the hell it came from. But since people do not believe in any inflow from heaven or from hell, and since then in their judgment everything they think and wish is within them, and therefore from them, they make the evil their own and defile with a sense of merit the good that flows in. (302)

The second excerpt's introductory phrase, "If people only believed," implies that there is a state in which we don't believe.

Thus, we must work on our disbelief before we can believe. Removing evils before doing good also obviously implies sequence. The dishonesty within us needs to be worked on before we can work on honesty. We have already seen through self-observation that we think that much of our lying and self-justification is honest when it is actually dishonest. We have to see our dishonesty before we can work on it. In the Work, some things necessarily must precede others.

The first thing we need to do is wake up. Awakening is a long process in the Work. We are asleep and dreaming that we are awake. We are among evils, but we are dreaming that we are good people. We awake when we observe our thoughts and feelings objectively, which lets us see things that we didn't previously see. For instance, in the task of observing our lying, we saw that we were lying, although that hadn't occurred to us before. The more awake we become, the more we can see: the relationship between self-observation and wakeful consciousness is progressive.

When we wake up and see the evils in ourselves, we find that we are identified with them. The next step is to learn not to identify with them. We see the evils for what they are — that IT is angry, IT is upset, IT is covetous — and we separate from them, pulling our feeling of who we are away from the part of us that is IT. It takes a great deal of effort to overcome our lying, justifying and rationalizing, and therefore learning not to identify is also a long process in the Work. We find that there are inherited things that are stuck to us and with which we are identified strongly. A television ad takes us underwater in our washing machine to show how the detergent breaks up the dirt and lifts it away. That is the feeling we want: we want to soak so long in self-observation that we see the evils clearly and can separate from them.

When we separate from IT, the Lord can flow in with good. Swedenborg says that we are in the stream of Providence when we trust in the Lord and see the Lord in everything. But we cannot simply declare, "Okay, I'm going to trust the Lord and see the Lord in everything, and I'll be right there in the stream of Providence." We must first become aware of what we do see in everything, and that we are in a state of *distrust*. When I am anxious about how a meeting will go, or worrying whether I will get there on time, do I trust the Lord? No. And it is that very state of distrust that stands in the way of my trusting, so *that* is what I work on. I cannot merely declare that I trust the Lord, but I can work on my distrust, and that work will lead to trusting the Lord.

Rather than seeing the Lord in everything, we see the world as screwed up, especially if, as is often the case, things don't go the way we want them to. We see *ourselves* in everything, not the Lord. What, then, do we work on? We work on not seeing ourselves in everything, and to the extent that we do not, we will see the Lord in all things. Swedenborg deals with these ideas in *Arcana Celestia*:

> All have the capacity to understand and to be wise but the reason one person is wiser than another is that they do not in like manner ascribe to the Lord all things of intelligence and wisdom, which are all things of truth and good. They who ascribe all to the Lord are wiser than the rest because all things of truth and good which constitute wisdom flow in from heaven, that is, from the Lord there. The ascription of all things to the Lord opens the interiors of man toward heaven, for thus it is acknowledged that nothing of truth and good is from himself, and in proportion as this is acknowledged and the love of self departs, and with the love of self the thick darkness from falsities and evils, in the same proportion man comes into innocence and into love and faith to the Lord from which comes conjunction with the Divine influx, thence enlightenment. (10227)

If only we would let go and discover the way things really are! If our minds were open and we took each day as it came, with trust in the Lord, we would see things differently. Because we cling so fervently to that which we understand, we make our world into a series of boring, repetitious events, whereas the world outside of us and the world within us is stupendous and incredible and ever new. Here is a story about trust, distrust and letting go of that to which we cling:

Once upon a time, long ago, there was a land of winged beings. These winged beings had human bodies, great gold wings and piercing blue eyes. They would fly high over the land, over mountains and rivers, waterfalls and lush forests. And the land below them was strewn with numberless beautiful gems of every color and description. In the sunlight, the gems sparkled and shone. The sight of them from high in the air was very, very beautiful. The winged beings loved flying and loved watching everything on the land below them, especially the sunlight sparkling on the crystalline jewels. And at night, the stars sparkled and the moon shone. The winged beings were the most contented creatures imaginable.

Then one day, one of the winged beings noticed a gem of extremely lovely color shining upward, and he had a feeling that he had never known before and said to himself, "I want that." He flew down and picked up the gem and had another feeling that he had never had before. As his hand closed tightly around the beautiful stone, he said, "This is *mine*."

Unfortunately, others saw him pick up the gem and hold it tightly. Before long, many winged beings were swooping to the ground, picking up jewels and flying off with them. Eventually, they weren't even seen in the air anymore; they were walking about the land, picking up gems and putting them in packs they had made for that purpose.

Soon, they were carrying so many precious jewels that they could not fly. In fact, they could hardly walk. After a while, they thought, "Maybe someone will take them." They retreated into caves and holes with their new possessions. They wouldn't venture very far from their caves because they were afraid that someone might take the gems that they now called their own.

Years passed. Generations proceeded. The winged beings now stayed in their caves. Their children had never seen a winged being fly! The new generations grew up in the caves, never went outside, never saw the sun and never flew. But the children were told that they were winged beings and that their great-great-grandparents had flown in the air above the land and had collected the gems, which they had left to their children and to their children's children.

The winged beings each had a pile of gems. They counted them and polished them — but, of course, the jewels didn't shine because there was no sunlight in the caves and the holes. But the winged beings imagined what it would be like if they took their jewels outside, how they would shine in the sunlight. They often imagined that and it made them feel very important and very wealthy.

Since they lived in caves and holes, the winged beings met the moles that lived under ground. The moles had no wings and their eyes were poor, so the winged beings felt very superior to them. Nonetheless, they spent a great deal of time telling the moles about the times when the heroes of their legends had found the tremendous piles of gems.

One day, a little mole and a very young winged being were talking. The mole said, "I know you have beautiful wings and piercing blue eyes. Will you tell me what it is like to fly?"

The winged being began, "My great-great-grandfather told me..."

The mole interrupted. "I don't want to know what your grandfather told you. I want to know what it feels like when you fly?" But the winged being answered that he really didn't know.

"I can't leave the cave to fly," the winged being said sadly, "because someone might take my possessions. These gems are mine."

"Well, then," said the mole, "you are not much better off than I am. You have good eyes, but you can't see, and you have wings, but you can't fly. At least I was made to live in the ground, but you were made to fly and to see, and you don't do either! You are worse off than I am. Why don't you fly and see?"

"Because I own these jewels and I don't want to lose them. Anyway, I don't know if we can still fly," explained the winged being.

A few days later, the winged being talked again with the little mole about almost never going outside his cave. Suddenly, he was aware of a new feeling — he wanted to go outside and he wanted to fly. But he also feared losing his gems. Nevertheless, one day, the young winged being poked his head out of his cave. He rubbed his eyes and looked around at the high, snow-capped mountains, the sapphire-blue sky and the crystal-clear water of a lake nearby. Slowly, cautiously, he emerged from his cave and stood for a few moments in the bright sunlight. Then, determinedly, he climbed a cliff, spread his golden wings, flapped them uncertainly a few times, leaped from the cliff and flew off through the air!

He was elated to be flying! As he flew and looked down at the land, now and then he heard a voice inside him say, "I want that." At those times, he flapped his wings a little harder and lifted himself higher because he remembered what it was like living in his dark cave, unable to see well or to use his wings except to cover and protect his unshining gems. Flying made him feel wonder at seeing far and wide over the land, watching the beautiful sunlight sparkling on the bright and lovely jewels.

One day, as the young being sat for a moment by a stream for a drink of clear water, another winged being crept watchfully out of a cave and quickly started picking up gems, putting them into a pack as he went.

"Why are you sitting out here by the stream?" the stealthy collector asked. "Don't you have any gems?"

"No," the young being said, "I don't think I do. I left them in my cave and I'm sure they have been taken by now."

"I have many gems," said the other. "Don't you want any?"

"No," the young being said, "I find that I don't need to have them for my own. Every day I play with many gems. I see the sunlight sparkling on them. I look at the world through them. Sometimes, I wash them in the stream, or make things out of them, but not to keep. The next day, I fly away and find new ones. Each day is a new experience."

Lifting his load of gems, the other said, "If you have nothing, then you are nothing. And if you think that way, then you think nothing. *You are nothing at all,*" he said, hurrying back to his cave.

The young being looked down at the stream. As he gazed, he focused carefully on the reflection of his face in the clear water. He smiled contentedly as he said to himself, "I am nothing." Then, still smiling, he rose, flapped his golden wings, and flew into the air, lifting himself higher and higher above the land.

A visualization may help us with our task. Closing our eyes, we become aware of where we are sitting, of our posture, of where our hands are, of whether our legs are crossed or uncrossed. Using our imagination, we draw our attention up toward the ceiling. From there, we look down on ourselves as we sit, seeing ourselves as clearly as possible. To do that, we can imagine looking at our back, or at our body's posture, or at the colors of our clothes. When we have a really clear image, we hold it in our imagination and remember that once there was a winged being who held onto his possessions in a dark cave.

When we find ourselves holding onto negative thoughts or feelings, we will do the task by drawing ourselves up and actually seeing ourselves having a negative experience. When we have drawn ourselves up and can see ourselves in that negative experience, we will remember the winged being, hiding in his dark cave, clinging to his possessions, and remember that when he gave up that to which he clung, he flew high above the land and clearly saw the beauty of the world.

THE TASK:

To pull our observing "I" out of ourselves and use it to observe ourselves during an active state of negative emotion, remembering the winged being hanging onto his possessions and flying once he let go.

7

"Minding" Our
Small "I's"

We have examined some of our big "I's" — contempt, anger, and the like. Let's now look at our small, petty "I's," and at the process we can call "minding."

Suppose that we've just spent a long weekend relaxing, while our kids came and went. Now, there are books on the floor, pillows thrown around, the couch pushed aside for a wrestling match, dirty dishes piled up here and there. The bathroom is a chaos of brushes and hair dryers and towels. The floor of the bedroom is cluttered with shoes, and discarded clothing is strewn everywhere. We decide to really clean up. We set a day aside and clean that house from top to bottom, which turns out to be a really big job.

Alternatively, we may choose to live in such a way that the need for a big housecleaning occurs less often. As we walk through the house, we pick up one pillow and throw it back on the couch. When we're done brushing our teeth, we put our toothbrush away. After eating, we put our dishes away and the milk back in the refrigerator. Every day. we do a little cleaning or straightening here and there as we go along. Consequently, there is an order in our house that doesn't exist if we let things pile up, then clean, then let things really pile up before we clean again. If we keep a certain amount of order, there is a certain tranquillity in our house.

Those small household disorders that constantly need a little cleaning up are analogous to the "I's" that just pop up and ruin a few minutes of our day. For instance, suppose that I'm waiting at a stoplight. As the light changes, I notice that the guy in the car in front of me is reading a book instead of paying attention to the traffic, and my emotional response is, "Aw, c'mon, man!" I can clean up that negative response with a little work, catching it half way and giving it up. Perhaps I come to the dinner table and notice that the rolls are there, but the butter is not — "Oh, no!" But I can let that go, too. Or, I go into the bathroom and find the hair dryer still plugged in and the water faucet still flowing. And so forth.

How can we have peace and tranquillity if our whole day is made up of a thousand petty, negative emotions? We can't. We cannot have peace and tranquillity if we hold on to even one of the negative emotions that keep popping up all day.

We may find it interesting to discover the smallest negative emotion, lasting the shortest time, that we can discern in ourselves, much as a wine-taster discriminates subtly among wines. Can we find an emotion of only one decibel, lasting only a third of a second, and really be aware of it? The Work tells us that a conscious person is aware of everything all the time. Even while walking down the street, doing nothing in particular, with no big, negative emotion happening, we must still pay attention.

What do we do with the nasty little negative blips that come and go? We just drop them. The moment we are aware of one, we just give it up. Are we hearing internal dialogue? We just shut it off, or we stop listening and turn our attention to something more important. It is only a little thing, so we just let it go and leave it alone.

We can refer collectively to all these little "I's" as "minding." Our minds adhere to certain forms, and we "mind" things because the world doesn't fit those forms. We think the world should go the way we like it, and we think that people should be the way we want them to be, that, for instance, they should always wear a coat and tie in church. Thus when a guy with purple hair and an earring comes into church wearing blue jeans, we "mind" that. Our mind holds a certain form, he doesn't fit the form, and we don't like it. What's worse, we think that the way we want it to be is the way it really should be. We can refer again to Nicoll's *Commentaries*:

> Now, how do you mind? Have you noticed how you mind things? Are you satisfied with how you mind things? Or might you mind things differently? To change the mind, new thoughts are necessary. We can notice that we mind things, but we do not connect that up with what kind of minds we have. In fact, we don't know that we have minds that have a particular form.

Our mental habits are to us not habits, but truths. They seem quite right to us. We cannot see them as habits and this is a tragedy.

The moving parts of centers are the lowest and most external parts of ourselves and here lie a great many small "I's" which only understand in a very small, limited way. When we live in these "I's," we are fast asleep as regards the Work.

We can think of the form of our mind as a cookie-cutter in the shape of that form. If we put our cookie-cutter over something its own shape, it won't "mind" at all, because the world seems just right. But the purple hair and jeans in church do not fit the cookie-cutter. The guy may have nice shoes that fit our form, and comb his hair, but the earring? We may really mind that, because it definitely does not fit the form. "That *earring* has got to go," our minding says. Anything that is not covered by our cookie-cutter is something we "mind," and which causes in us a negative response.

If we are aware, we will observe these negative emotions, or little minding "I's." If something doesn't fit the way our mind is formed, we mind it, not because that thing is inappropriate, but because our mind has such an oddly specific, cookie-cutter shape. We inherited that shape, and many of the things we experience just do not fit it.

Consequently, we often think of something as presenting a moral question when it simply does not. Historically, for instance, we find that certain things, about which morally we once felt very strongly, are not moral questions at all. They are just matters of minding. In Shakespeare's time, if a woman played the role of a woman in a play, it was a moral outrage. Men had to dress up like women to play their roles. Today, if a man dresses like a woman to play a woman's part, we may worry about it, or maybe even "mind" it, but it is not a moral issue for us.

Of course, if someone commits murder, we should mind. But we are not talking about situations like that. We are talking about observing that the cause of our negative emotions is often the very limited shape of our mind. Nonetheless, there are certain things that will never change, like the need to obey the Ten Commandments. If we disobey the Ten Commandments, we should mind. But the other five hundred commandments that we also think should have been written in stone, we can give up. At least we might want to think about them and reconsider. For now, we will just observe.

We will observe our minding. We will notice what we mind and how often we are minding. We will also look for the quietest, smallest "I," the subtlest, shortest-lived negative feeling that we can identify. We will notice our minding as in the beam of a flashlight shone into a room. We don't have to clean the room yet; we will just shine the light in there and notice what is going on. Nicoll writes, in *Commentaries*:

> If you understand the direction of the Work, then whatever happens in life will not destroy you. You will not be surprised at what happens in life because you will know that life is like that, that man cannot do, and success and failure in life will mean less and less to you. You will not expect life to give you what only the Work can give you.

When self-observation begins to accompany you, you will notice that it is not critical. It is simply a slight degree of consciousness, an awareness. Through this awareness, you simply see more. This awareness does not accuse you, it merely shows you what is going on inside yourself.

THE TASK:

(1) To observe our minding of people, things and events;

(2) To identify the smallest, subtlest negative emotion that we can perceive.

8

True Conscience and Spiritual Growth

The Work tells us that negative emotions can never see the truth that positive emotions can see. If we are in a negative state, we cannot see the truth of what is going on because we are emotionally in a society from hell; that is where our spirit is and we cannot see truth from there — we can see only one side of it.

While in a negative state, we can ask ourselves, "Does my proprium really care?" Perhaps IT cares only about the emotion IT is stirring in us. For example, my family was on the way to a Thanksgiving service. I was ready to go, but the others were not, and I was getting impatient and upset. Suddenly, it occurred to me to ask if my proprium really cared whether IT got to church on time. IT didn't care at all! IT wasn't even going to church! IT had simply seen an opportunity to express impatience by getting me to identify with IT.

On another occasion, I was watching T.V. downstairs. I was comfortable down there, but then the kids wanted to watch that T.V. I went back upstairs, huffing and puffing in annoyance. Then I asked, "Is my proprium even watching T.V.?" The answer was no — IT could not have cared less. Did IT care what I or the kids watched? Not at all. All IT cared about was the opportunity to bring me into a society from hell and get me to identify with ITS negative emotions. If we are unaware, IT will use any situation as a justification for entering us. Nicoll reminds us of another aspect of negative emotions, in Commentaries:

> Negative emotions have their own kind of knowledge,
> particularly in regard to how to hurt people and wound
> them. When you are in a negative state toward some-

one, you know, as a rule, how to most hurt that person and say wounding things. When followed, these emotions lead to hell. In every case, negative emotions can only see half the truth.

When we let negative emotions stay around, we call them "I" because we are identified with them. When an angry spirit is present, we say, "I'm angry." However, when we use the word "I," we should think of a state, or, actually, of a spirit, and be aware that an entire spiritual society can be manifest in the single spirit that is with us. That one spirit is in touch with an entire society and represents that society in us by acting as one of our "I's." About these "I's," Nicoll writes:

> What is an "I?" An "I" is a definite personality in us, a small being with an intellectual, emotional, and moving part. You must understand that "I's" are quite real people in you. On one occasion, Ouspensky said, "You all think that these 'I's' are not real. I assure you that they are quite real and live in the house of your own being, and they continually try to control you."

Often, it is conscience that calls us away from a negative state. Although we have heard of conscience throughout our lives, we may be unfamiliar with its different forms. The Work mentions "acquired conscience," which in the Writings is called "spurious conscience." The Work speaks of "real conscience," which in the Writings is called "true conscience." There is also "false conscience," which is discussed repeatedly in both systems. Swedenborg writes of the three forms of conscience in *Arcana Celestia*:

> Conscience in general is either true, spurious, or false. A *true conscience* is that which is formed by the Lord from the truths of faith, and when a man is endowed with it, he is afraid to act against the truths of faith, for thus he would act against conscience. No one can receive this conscience who is not in the truths of faith, and few in the Christian world are. Nevertheless, they who are being regenerated receive conscience together with charity, for charity is the fundamental of conscience.

A *spurious conscience* is that which is formed with the gentiles from their religion and religious worship in which they have been born and educated, to act against which is to them to act against conscience. When their conscience is founded in charity and mercy and obedience, they are then those who can receive a true conscience in the other life.

A *false conscience* is that which is formed not from internal but from external things, that is, not from charity but from the love of self and the world. There are some who seem to themselves to be acting against conscience when they are acting against the neighbor, and who also at such times seem to themselves to be inwardly tortured, but it is because they perceive in thought that their own life, honor, reputation, wealth and gain, are in danger. (1033)

Each of us probably has these three forms of conscience. A true understanding of them allows us to give what is called a sensory-based description of them, that is, to talk about the differences between true conscience and false conscience and to define them with examples. On the other hand, if we can't distinguish between them in ourselves on a sensory, or experiential, basis, it is very difficult to allow one kind of conscience to lead us and to separate from the other. How can we know which one to separate from and which one to follow unless we have identified, from experience, which is which? Conscience is very necessary, and we must experience it rather than just thinking about it.

True conscience is a fear of going against the truths of the Word that have been learned. After I stopped drinking a few years ago, I had a scary experience: I had a dream in which I had a drink. It frightened me. I awoke in a sweat and was really scared. It wasn't a fear that I was going to get caught; it was a fear that I had done something contrary to a direction in which I really wanted to move. I believe that is the kind of fear of which the Writings speak.

Spurious conscience is potentially true, but founded on something that is not from the Lord and not truly doctrinal, such as the Victorian imperative that dresses had to be worn down to the ankles. People even may have thought that it was a religious teaching, and, therefore, that wearing dresses down to the ankles was an issue of religious morality. If, on a beautiful day, a woman indulged an urge to lift her dress up over her knees and run through a lovely meadow, she might have had a pang of conscience, spurious conscience, about going against something the church taught. Perhaps, in fact, it was not so taught, but she thought it was, and she was struggling with what she considered to be a moral teaching of the church. Such struggles can lead to true conscience, as long as our motive is to do what is good.

False conscience is also based on fear, but it is the fear that comes from the "eleventh commandment," which is made up by people: thou shalt not get caught. Getting caught is what the proprium, from false conscience, fears. It is the fear of losing our honor or reputation or material gain through getting caught. Consider our fear of committing adultery. We may be afraid of getting caught. That is false conscience. On the other hand, we may be afraid of injuring the relationship that is the most important thing in our life. That is more likely real conscience. If we have a true love for the Lord and for the neighbor, we really are frightened that our proprium may do something contrary to the loves we are learning. We are afraid that IT may take us over and go against what we are struggling toward. I think that is the fear of real conscience, while the fear of getting caught is false conscience.

The Writings emphasize how important it is to go to the Word ourselves to determine what the Lord wishes us to do. Finding for ourselves what is true in the Word takes us from spurious conscience (what we *think* the church and others have taught us) to real conscience. When we find by ourselves that which is true, we feel that the Lord has told us what we should fear to go against. The Work tells us never to take anything for granted, always to verify everything ourselves, and never to trust anything we read or hear. That is the same advice given by the Writings: don't settle for spurious conscience — develop true conscience from one's own understanding of the Word.

What is our experience? Can we differentiate between the fear of going against a truth that we really believe the Lord teaches (that is, the fear of hurting the Lord) and the fear of getting caught? Can we describe the difference between those two fears? How are we able to distinguish the two in everyday life?

For instance, false conscience does cause us to feel that we are acting against conscience, but we know that it is false conscience when we realize that we would act if we knew we would not get caught, or if we knew our action would not affect our reputation. True conscience is an internal process, but being internal doesn't guarantee that a process is true conscience. There is a stage, between a concern for ourselves and true conscience, in which we are motivated by a fear of going to hell, or by a wish to go to heaven. The transition from false conscience to true conscience is gradual — one is not suddenly just replaced by the other.

We need to practice distinguishing between true and false conscience, to examine our experience to find how they feel different. The words we use to describe them must become concepts that we can actually work with and live by. The struggle of false conscience is described in a sermon by Geoffrey Childs about King Saul in a state of torment:

> To sit captive by the River of Babylon is to be enslaved by the rivers of self-love and ambition and self-glory. To weep is to feel genuine sorrow for this captivity, to wish to leave it without having the strength to do so. In this slave state, how can we sing the Lord's song? Nor, in this state, much as we may want to, can we confess the Lord. To confess the Lord is to play the vibrant, haunting strings of the harp. This harp will remain silent in the strange land of dominion by desire.
>
> The spirit of the Lord departed from Saul and an evil spirit troubled him. Saul, the first king of Israel, represents the outer conscience. This conscience is based not upon the truth, but upon a person's desire to appear good before others. Before repentance, this is the conscience that rules, and a person has no idea that it is superficial or unsound. For years, Saul was the king of Israel. But the time comes when we may see the external conscience for what it is, and we see that it is inadequate to fight real evil. We cannot rid ourselves of our false external conscience all in a moment. Saul remained the ruler of Israel despite the anointing of David. Early in spiritual life, it is the best conscience we can have and, despite its selfish nature, the Lord is with it.
>
> When internal truth is anointed and loved, then the desire to please others for the sake of honor becomes

wrong. The spirit of the Lord departs from Saul. There are times when, despite our desire to serve spiritual truth, we find ourselves troubled by evil emotions. Therefore, Saul sent a messenger to Jesse and said, "Send me your son David who is with the sheep." When David played upon the harp before Saul, the torment that ravaged Saul ceased. The same thing may occur with us when our spirit is troubled by the tumult of external ambitions or desires. We can open our hearts to the song of David. This inner affection of truth can come down and bring peace even to our external emotions. The pure affection of truth is the mother of our genuine love to the Lord.

Affection for truth opens the way to true conscience. Self-observation, the rational part of the mind, has an affection for truth for truth's sake. As we move away from the proprium, away from worldly desires, we have a different affection, the affection of observing and trying to understand what is going on. Affection for truth makes us wonder what is happening within us spiritually. We ask, "How does it happen that looking at a certain thing suddenly produces a negative emotion?" We find that we have a real desire to know and understand IT. Then, separation from IT can take place. We draw who we are up to a spiritual point of view and look down on our life from this new affection for truth.

When we talked about "minding," we discussed our need to have the world fit the cookie-cutter form of our mind. "First force" is that desire for the world to go the way we want it to go, and for people to be the way we want them to be. "Second force" is resistance, when the world doesn't go the way we want it to, producing in us a negative reaction. To counter second force, we apply self-observation, separation, and the other tools of the Work. That application of the Work to resistance is "third force." We bring the Work to the resistance, seeing the world and everything in it from the perspective of the Work. Third force is knowing, believing, and living the truth that the way things are is perfect. The Lord's plan gives us exactly what we need to work on.

First force can be called desire, or wanting. We have two main loves, love of the world and love of self. Love of the world is wanting the world to be a certain way — we want a certain house, we want a certain car, we want a certain amount of money. Love of self is wanting people to be the way we want them to be. It is love of dominion — they better do what we tell them; those kids had better behave, or else.

However, second force is not always present. Sometimes, we want things to go our way, and they do — I want a promotion, and I get one. In that case, I may be unaware of the negative emotion of wanting things to go my way. I may not even notice my wanting because nothing gets in its way. We must observe in ourselves the negative "wanting" emotions that are hidden in the sense that they have not yet bumped into second force.

We have also spoken of loves, or desires, that are compatible with the process of regeneration and of loves that are not. Loves derived from the covetousness described in the Ninth and Tenth Commandments are incompatible with regeneration — coveting the very house that belongs to someone else, for example. On the other hand, wanting a house like someone else's, or just wanting a *nice* house, may be compatible with regeneration. Likewise, love of dominion is incompatible, whereas love of good management, or love of organization in pursuit of a good purpose, may be compatible. The loves that are incompatible with regeneration are the ones to which we must directly apply the Work.

The Writings tell us that we can love riches, fine houses, and nice gardens, because wanting them can be compatible with eternal life. What makes our wanting incompatible? In the case of riches, the Writings tell us that we can have them, but "do not put your heart on them." We must not put our heart where our treasure is, where moth and rust corrupt. Although wanting can be compatible with regeneration, most of our desires, being from the proprium, are evil, as Swedenborg shows in *Arcana Celestia*:

> So long as the desires of evil block up the interior of the natural mind, man is in hell, but as soon as these desires are dispersed by the Lord, he is then in heaven.

> To covet what belongs to the neighbor is also contrary to the disposition of those who are in charity. The desires of the world must be put off, and the affections of heaven must be put on. (1798)

Nicoll makes a similar point in *Commentaries:*

Have you ever examined your internal man and perceived any desires? Must not the desires which hold each other by the hands and so sport, be first removed and new desires which are good and truth, be introduced in the place of these cupidities which are of evil and falsity? That these things cannot be done in a moment every wise man sees from this alone, that evil is composed of innumerable desires, wherefore, unless one evil is brought forth after another and this until their connection is broken up, man cannot be made new.

To make ourselves new, one of our tasks consists of identifying our desires, and learning what they feel like, without their being made apparent by the presence of second force, and then working on them directly, before they encounter second force. How do we do that? We bring third force, or the effort of the Work, directly to our experience of those desires.

For instance, if we plan an outdoor wedding and want it to go our way in the form of nice weather, if second force arrives on the day of the wedding in the form of rain, we will have a negative response. But if, in our planning, we acknowledge second force as a possibility and, further, use third force to accept that the Lord is in charge of the weather, then we will hold our desire very lightly. We will not allow our heart to dwell upon a sunny day for the wedding, since, in our very desire for good weather, we have accepted whatever actually happens as the Lord's doing.

We can think again of my hope for a promotion. I do, in fact, hope for promotion, but I don't set my heart on it. I acknowledge second force, the possibility that I may not be promoted, and use third force, praying, "not my will, but Yours be done." In this way, I hold the desire for promotion with all three forces present. Then, if I do not get the promotion, I may experience disappointment, but not rage or bitterness.

What we are doing is holding the world and its material things in proper proportion. We are holding the Lord's Providence, the way things are and will be, higher than our own will, higher than our wants and our delights. Through the Work, we separate from, or subdue, our desire and refuse to dwell upon our hope for its fulfillment.

We are allowed to experience the delights of the world. We may enjoy a fine house, a nice vacation, a delicious meal, and we may look forward to a sports event or party that we plan to attend. But we do not hold our delights in such a way that, if second force comes along and prevents us from having them as we expected, we are going to get into a negative state. A positive emotion cannot be turned into its opposite. If we are holding our delights in such a way that they don't turn into strong negative emotions, then they are ordered correctly. In the heavens, love of the Lord and of the neighbor make the head, while love of self makes the soles of the feet. Can we consciously hold the affections that enter us in such a way that they are at the level of our feet? If we do, negativity will not arise in relation to many natural delights and, in this way, our desires can be compatible with spiritual growth.

My father once said to me, "You will know you are in heaven if, when you drive to church late, you find all the parking spots in front of church available because the people who got there earlier knew that they had more time to walk than the people who would come late." That is a description of the change that takes place when we work. If we watch our desires, we can catch the little ones. When we want the best parking space, we can recognize that as a selfish desire.

Do we want to get the window-seat on the train? Do we want the biggest piece of pie? We must consciously identify those wants because there is no other way for us to make such desires passive before they are met by second force and produce negativity. The early angel who leaves the closest parking spaces available once identified with the feeling of wanting the best parking space, but observed and separated from IT, putting charity above wanting the best spot. But the angel had to consciously identify the experience of that desire before being able to separate from IT.

We certainly can look forward to a vacation in the Bahamas, and even anticipate nice weather. But if it rains and we feel disappointed, at what point does our negativity become inappropriate? The Writings tell us that a person in the stream of Providence remains unruffled whether she gains riches or loses them. If she is poor, she is unruffled because she knows the Lord is mindful of her eternal welfare. Swedenborg gives a beautiful description of a person holding wealth very lightly. But such an attitude does not just happen naturally. We must go through some conscious changes to be able to live that way in regard to riches, since, in our experience, we also know of the man who lost five million of his eight million dollars when the market went down and saw fit to shoot both his stockbroker and himself. Our response to things depends upon how we hold them.

We want to be aware of how we are holding things, of our wants and desires, and of how our attitude changes depending upon what happens to our wants and desires. What is our experience of putting our heart on things? How do we do that? How long may we dwell upon something before we have put our heart on it? Are we able to just touch our desire, then let it go real fast because we do not want to put our heart on it? Our task involves observing our desires, being aware of what we want, and noticing where our desires enter our body.

In *Spiritual Diary,* Swedenborg often speaks of "a certain society" attacking his stomach, or of experiencing influx as pain in his left shoulder. As we identify those small desires that come in the form of "I want...," or "I am looking forward to...," or "I can't wait for...," we can also observe their physical sensations. We can notice where we actually experience our desires physically, where they enter our body, especially if we concentrate on one particular desire at a time. We cannot know that we are having an emotion unless we experience it, and we will experience it somewhere in our body. We want to observe two types of desire: one is compatible with regeneration, depending upon how we hold it; the other is absolutely contrary to spiritual growth.

THE TASK:

(1) To experience our small wants or desires and, if possible, to identify where particular ones enter our body;

(2) To observe, if we wish, how we hold a desire, and to see if we can determine whether it is compatible or incompatible with regeneration.

9

THE WHOLE
NINE STEPS

The Work instructs us that one of our very first tasks is to become passive to life. This is a very difficult thing to understand because we think that we can do and because we always think that things should be different than they are. We know the steps of regeneration, or actual repentance, as described in the Writings. We know what we should do, and why we should do it, but we need to learn more about *how* to do it. Nicoll provides a clue:

> You cannot change yourself if you take yourself as yourself, and all attempts to do this will lead into a dangerous situation. You have to be able to say to yourself, "I am not this 'I,' I am not this thought that comes to me, I will not take pleasure in thinking or feeling in this way."

If our car were not really running very well, a friend might say to us, "You know, that car of yours could be really useful if it could be driven. You should fix it." And we might well agree that something needed to be done, even though we might not know exactly what to do. That is like the situation in which we find ourselves: we should fix ourselves, but how do we actually go about doing it? It involves more than just knowing that we should do it. We need to look at how to actually go about getting fixed.

There are various ways to describe the process of regeneration: Some people say there are three steps, some seven, some ten. We will talk about nine steps. As we do, we will notice that the steps are interrelated, that each step appears to produce the next step and to be a natural outgrowth of the preceding step.

The first step is to know about evils. If we decide to fix our car, we must know something about what makes an engine run well and what makes one run badly, and we can gain that knowledge only through study and understanding. Only then can we approach the job of fixing our car with some probability of having it work well. In the process of regeneration, we gain our knowledge from revelation, from studying the Word, from parents and teachers, and from other sources. Knowledge is the first step.

The second step is to observe ourselves from the knowledge we have gained from revelation and learning. But we cannot observe ourselves from the natural mind because we are identified with our natural mind, and it is in our natural mind that all our evils and natural inclinations exist. But we know from the Writings and the Work that we have a rational mind that is higher than the natural mind. The second step of repentance requires us to raise ourselves up into our rational mind so that we can look down and observe what is going on in the natural mind below.

This is a very important step. It is the self-observation of the Work, done without criticism, without identification, and with inner separation. It is not merely thinking, once or twice a year, about what we may have done wrong. It is the self-examination that we must practice at the time that an evil occurs, not from within the evil itself, but from the rational above it. In accord, the Writings teach that we have the ability to raise our conscious thought from the lower regions of our mind into the higher regions, or into the light of heaven. It is while thinking from the internal of thought that we have the ability to examine the influx of ideas that are present in the lower regions of our mind. Self-examination is the second step of repentance.

Self-observation leads naturally to the third step: recognizing evils in ourselves. When we raise ourselves up into our internal, rational mind and observe, from doctrine or from the Work, what is going on below, we see things that we have never seen before. In our task on lying, it surprised us to find how much we lied. In the exercise on experiencing contempt, we were surprised at how contemptuous our natural mind is. The false personality that thinks we are a nice person because we do not overtly break any of the Ten Commandments disappears during active self-examination, as we recognize evils in the self and see that things that we thought were good, because we rationalized them as allowable, are in fact evil. And evil is not justified. To see the evils in ourselves is the third step.

In the fourth step, we acknowledge that these evils are in the self. The appearance is that our negative emotions are caused by things in the external world. The truth is that the causes are within us. It only appears to us that our anger is caused by the person driving slowly in front of us when we are in a hurry. And there are plenty of "appearances" for the hells to use against us. But the causes of our anger, frustration, jealousy, irritation, and impatience are not outside us, and our conviction that they are outside us is one of our major illusions. There is something "out there," such as the person driving slowly, that evil spirits use to justify and blame. But through self-examination, we see that the cause of our anger is in us, from hell, although we are not the cause. Our anger is hereditary in the proprium, which justifies ITs existence by saying that the fellow who drives too slowly causes our anger. Nonetheless, not everyone behind the slow driver gets angry, so how could he be the cause? Acknowledging that evil is within us is the fourth step. Swedenborg writes in *Arcana Celestia*:

> In this last phase of the third step of actual repentance as well as the beginning of the fourth step, man finds himself in one of the lowest spiritual states imaginable. He sees himself as nothing but filthiness and blackness, for he is then in annihilation of self, nay, in the loathing of self. Repentance is not possible without this state of humiliation, for without it man is not able to look to or be receptive of the Lord. (3994)

However, the Work reminds us to ask *which* self we are loathing. There is a real difference between "loathing of self" that is the proprium, and loathing of self in the belief that we *are* the proprium.

The fifth step is to make ourselves guilty. The sixth step is to condemn ourselves. We see the evils that are in us, we make ourselves guilty, and we condemn ourselves for those evils. Again the Work helps us by demonstrating that the self that is guilty is the proprium. IT is guilty. IT is prone to all those evils. IT has made new evils. IT justifies and rationalizes. IT *is* guilty.

In one sense, we are our proprium. We are born with IT and from that time IT strives within us from the deepest hells toward evils of every kind. Fortunately, we are not our proprium in terms of who we are potentially — we are only vessels. Our present will may be evil and our understanding false, but we are created in such a way that the Lord can give us a new rational and a new will formed within that rational. We must identify with who we are potentially — the rational, the Work "I's," the part that will be cleansed and made new — rather than with the proprium, which will never change.

When we believe ourselves to be the proprium, everything we fear is confirmed: we are helpless, hopeless, and condemned. We are in our natural mind, identified with all the proprium's evil loves and nasty thoughts. We want them to stop, but they don't, and we may be tempted to give up. This is because we are not in our rational mind, where uncritical and nonidentified self-observation makes possible what is virtually impossible without it. There is no use in condemning ourselves if we condemn the wrong part. It is the evil proprium that we must condemn, rather than identifying with IT.

Thus we pull ourselves up into the rational, where the *potential* us will be born, and look down on the *hereditary* us: the proprium, guilty and condemned. The greater our separation and the more objective our self-observation, the more clearly we see that the proprium can never go to heaven, for IT strives against all the Lord's efforts to regenerate us, to take us out of IT and to make IT passive.

Step seven is the confession of our evils before the Lord. We lay out the evils we see, honestly and completely. We tell the Lord where in our body we feel them. We reveal all our thoughts and emotions about the evils we see. We open up our evils to the Lord as much as we are able and say, "This is what I see." We confess to the Lord in *detail*. It is not just a matter of admitting, "I am a sinner." We must stay aware and confess everything we can find, the little things and the big things. In detail.

Over time, we observe ourselves being slaves, being mechanical, unable to free ourselves from the proprium, even though we see ITs behavior and recognize the damage IT does. Over and over again, we believe IT, act from IT, and justify IT. Then we wake up and say, "Oh, no, I did it again!" Seeing this pattern in ourselves, we want a closer relationship with the Lord. The eighth step of regeneration is to pray to the Lord for help. We pray because we realize it is the only way out. Only the Lord can free us and save us.

We can recognize that in the first seven steps, we are praying to the Lord. We are using conscious effort to raise ourselves up, to observe evils, to acknowledge that they are evil, to see that they are in us, to see that their cause is in us, to declare the proprium guilty and condemned, and to confess our evils to the Lord. That effort is inner prayer. However, the verbal prayer of the eighth step follows the Work we do in the preceding steps.

Step nine, the final step in the series, is to desist from evils. The first eight steps produce in us a closer relationship with the Lord, making it possible for the first time for us to actually resist evils. With the birth of a new will from the Lord, evil can be made passive. We draw up above our proprium and the new will is made active in the rational.

The Writings teach us that an evil that is resisted eventually will be put to the side. It will never be done away with, but it is put to the outer edge. We may still be aware of it, or we may not be; it is still there, but not in the center of our consciousness. The hells are still there, but they are farther away from us and passive. Our essence, or good loves, is now active in our center. The new will is being born. As the new will is formed, we more and more dislike that which IT likes and like that which IT dislikes. We develop an affection for the truth and for the good within the truth. We actually feel pleasure in doing good things. But we cannot feel such pleasure when we are identified with the active proprium. It is first necessary that we desist from evil, both the external behaviors forbidden by the Ten Commandments and the more internal evils in which we engage in our minds. Desisting from evil is step nine.

We may perform all of these regenerative steps in the space of a second in relation to one negative emotion. For instance, while driving by someone's house, all of a sudden we find that we covet it. If we are awake, we draw ourselves up, we observe our desire, we see that it is evil, we see that it is in us, we see that it is condemned, we ask the Lord for help, we desist from it, and we think about something else. All that can happen very fast.

However, our fight against our covetousness may occur in this way again and again for a long, long time. It may be twenty years before we arrive at a state in which we do not experience that covetousness, and in which we begin to experience a new life. We may well wonder what is actually happening in the spiritual world while here on earth we are coveting that house and then deciding to work on our negative response. What happens may be something like this:

We here on earth see that house. We have an evil, proprial

reaction: we want that house. By that mechanical, proprial wanting, our inclination to covet, we invite closer to us those spiritual societies that are also into coveting. But if we decide to do the Work and to go through the steps of repentance, we raise ourselves up into the rational and look down and see the nature of our covetousness. We notice where we feel it physically, what it says, and what thoughts go along with it. If we have an affection for understanding what is going on, then that affection for the truth brings a good society toward us. As that good society comes closer, we feel in ourselves a separation occurring between ITs covetousness and the love of truth. As the affection for truth comes closer yet, the covetousness moves away, which is inner separation. Eventually, the evil inclination becomes passive.

The affection for knowing what is going on spiritually results in greater separation, because simply knowing, or even suspecting, that there are spiritual societies around us as we work is a tremendous help. The slightest advantage over an evil will lead to salvation, if we persist. At first, it may be only a decrease in our delight in the evil. But that is a positive step away from our former state. To recognize that we take delight in an evil is to take less delight in it than we did before that recognition.

When we are totally in the delight of some negative habit or attitude, we simply accept it. But if we have reflected upon it at all, when it recurs we are less than totally involved. A little piece of us is gradually changing. A little seed is growing when we say, "I know I'm doing it, but it is wrong." That little part will gradually grow because we acknowledge the negative, see and admit that IT is damaging, that IT is condemned, and that IT enjoys evil. That little part is the potential us that can be changed, even though IT can never be changed.

Although regeneration is a very individual thing, the support of others who are working can be of considerable encouragement — when I fall asleep, someone else in my group may be awake. But we must be cautious because our proprium likes to take credit by appearing to be part of a movement, when all IT wants is to ridicule something. In the Work, this is called taking the Work on a formatory level. When we start the Work, we have a tendency to talk about it on an ordinary level, especially with people who are also in the Work. We may greet our spouse by saying, "Boy, aren't you identified today!" We must not do this. The proprium is trying to destroy our growing relationship with the Lord by reducing the

Work to the level of jokemaking. Hell aims to make the Work totally ineffective by keeping it on a natural level, and we feel that inclination. When we are in the Work, it is best not to talk about it to people who are not in the Work. At times, it is wise not to talk about the Work even to those who are in the Work.

It is a powerful experience to see an organization fail, or to watch a church die. The principles that were once so important are taken on a formatory level and used by the proprium. The organization loses its power because there is no longer an inner drive — the proprium has appropriated the principles to ITSELF. We must watch our proprium. We must not not let IT talk for us. IT is not in the Work. We are trying to separate from IT. When IT pretends that IT is in the Work, and we are seduced by that pretense, we give away the power that can save us.

In *Arcana Celestia.*, Swedenborg describes when we are responsible for our state:

> Man is not to be held responsible for those thoughts
> which flow into his mind from angelic or infernal spir-
> its, but only for those thoughts which he chooses to
> entertain in the will. Evil enters into the will by being
> kept in the thought by consent and especially by act,
> and the consequent delight. (6204)

As we learn that we are not condemned for thoughts that do not enter our will, we need to find out which thoughts do enter our will. What is the experience of thought entering the will? How long do we have a thought in mind before we experience it entering into the will? How do we get rid of the thought, or stop thought, before it enters our will? If it does enter the will, what do we do with it? Some of these questions are answered in *Divine Providence*:

> Nothing is appropriated to man that he merely thinks,
> or even that he thinks to will, unless at the same time he
> wills it to such a degree as to do it when the opportunity
> offers. (80)

This gives rise to powerful and useful questions to ask as we observe our thoughts and behavior. We may have a thought about something negative, but if we had the opportunity, would we do it? If, for instance, we are struggling on a natural level with a diet, how long do we think about breaking it before we do break it?

Can we get rid of the thought before then?

Our current task is the "after-image" task. If we look at a bright light for a count of ten, then close our eyes, we see an after-image of the light until it fades. It is fairly easy to discern that the after-image is not the light, and that the light is not the after-image. But we will not have the after-image unless we have looked at the light, so the light, in a way, produces the after-image. However, even if the light goes out when we close our eyes, we will still have the after-image.

Nicoll writes that when we see something we do not like, we experience dislike. That is different than *thinking about* disliking someone or something. Thinking about our dislike is the after-image. There is little we can do about the experience of dislike because it is mechanical. It comes very quickly and almost automatically. We can, however, work on the after-image of thinking about disliking.

The task is to be aware of a negative emotion or thought and to pay attention to its after-image. How much of our experience is an immediate, negative reaction? How much is after-image? How long does the after-image last? It may fade only slowly if we pay attention to it, or faster if we turn our attention elsewhere. We can do some beneficial Work with our after-images, whereas we cannot work on our emotions themselves. We cannot decide simply that "Every time I see So-and-So, I'm going to love him." It just does not happen that way. When we see So-and-So, we may feel contempt. But if we are conscious, we can shorten the after-image. We do not have to entertain our negative thoughts. Our task is to identify the difference between experiencing a negative emotion and entertaining negative thoughts in an "after-image."

THE TASK:

(1) To notice a negative emotion and pay attention to the after-image. How much of the negative is immediate reaction and how much is after-image?

(2) To notice whether the after-image fades faster if we focus on it or turn away from it.

1 0

Short-form Repentance, or What the Proprium Doesn't Know

As we progress in the Work, we put the feeling of "I" into that part of us that chooses to work and to become obedient to the internal. We gradually withdraw the feeling of who we are from false personality, or the proprium. In *Commentaries*, Nicoll gives a good summary of what the Work is about:

> When you are in a state of real self-observation, you can see different "I's" trying to take hold of you. You want to sit down or you want to rest, you want to eat or you want to smoke, you want to listen to some negative "I's," you want to feel depressed, you want to feel bored, you want to feel wrong, you want to find fault, or you want to hurt somebody, or you want to get into a temper. You hear all these different "I's" speaking all around you, and probably many others, and you say "No" to them all. All these "I's" wish you to say "Yes" to them and to consent to what they suggest.

> A man or a woman can undergo a definite development by giving up what they have come to think they are. This is where self-observation starts. It is your own life-built personality that must be observed by each of you until something separates from it. This thing that separates is what can grow. The method of this gradual shifting of the feeling of oneself begins with observation of oneself, noticing oneself. It does not begin with going against oneself. How can you go against something which you do not know? It is necessary to begin with

self-observation. This ray of light, this ray of consciousness arising from noticing oneself, begins to enter into
this darkness, this ignorance of ourselves, and very
slowly brings about a change.

The Writings mention an easier kind of repentance than the
nine steps of regeneration we have just discussed. We could probably use this easier kind of repentance on some of our states,
although on others of our states we would have to use the nine
steps, or what we might call the "long form." Swedenborg
describes the "short form" in *True Christian Religion*:

When anyone is giving thought to any evil and intending it, he shall say to himself, Although I am thinking
about this and intending it, I will not do it because it is a
sin. By this means the temptation from the hells is
checked and its further entrance is prevented. (535)

Now that sounds pretty easy until we imagine sitting in a chair,
with our feet not touching the floor, and trying to move the chair
without getting up. The chair cannot be moved from that position,
can it? We need to get up in order to move the chair. The spot on
which we place our feet in assuming the position necessary to
move the chair is analogous to the rational.

This analogy sheds light on our efforts to repent. We cannot
look at the proprium from *within* the proprium, just as we cannot
move the chair if we have no place to stand *apart from* the chair.
We must have a place to step to in order to allow change in ourselves. Our proprium does not change, but from the rational we
can see the proprium and separate from IT, or change our position,
and act from higher influences. But we must alter our viewpoint,
or our position, before anything new or different can happen. That
place to step to, that separation, is vital.

The place that we can step to is our thinking from the things
we have learned from doctrine, which are the truths and the goods
in the rational. It is there that we put our feeling of who we are, so
that no matter what is going on, we are observing from the Work.
How do we do that? We move ourselves into the truth, into doctrine, into the rational, and look down on what the proprium is
doing, rather than being identified with the proprium.

If we make that inner separation even momentarily, but in that
moment we see that IT is down there, then we are off the chair for

that moment and it is possible to move the chair. This experience is entirely different from our theoretical knowledge that there is a rational wherein there is truth, without actually having the feeling of being there. Our first efforts to remember ourselves and to elevate our thinking are just intellectual practice.

Before we have elevated our thinking and our feeling of "I," while we are still identified with our proprium below, we will do whatever we intend at the earliest opportunity, as long as we know how to do it. Identification with our proprium results automatically in mechanical, proprial behavior. But there is an interesting thing about influx. Although spirits flow into our thought and will and thereby stir our affections to do something, they do not flow into our speech or action, since that would constitute external possession, which is no longer permitted. There is a "break" between our thinking about something, our willing or intending it, and our doing it. In that break is the possibility of not doing it. What we are considering is that position from which we are not going to act. If we are thinking of and intending something, and have the opportunity to act, why don't we?

For instance, at a party someone says to John Doe, "Did you hear that Sally and Edgar split up?" John Doe responds, "No kidding? They've been married for ten years. It's sad. I don't understand it. But I did see Edgar out walking with his secretary last week. Remember the way he was in high school? It's just like him to get involved with someone else, you know? Actually, it's not so surprising after all. He really is that way."

Can John Doe use the short form of repentance? Before he can decide not to act, John first has to be capable of enough self-observation to see that he is thinking evil. Further, he must have enough information from the Work to decide what is or is not evil. Has John identified his remarks as evil? Does he see his comments as sin? Is it clear to him that his talk might do damage to Edgar or Sally or both? Does he understand that his slander is rooted in hatred and contempt? If John does not see these things clearly, how can he work? He cannot.

Swedenborg's short form begins, "When anyone is giving thought to an evil and intending it..." Does John have enough self-observation to realize that he may have held his thought long enough for it to have gone into his will? An awareness that one's thought has gone into one's will is implicit in the words "although I am thinking about it, and intending it, I will not do it." John's ability to "say to himself" in the way Swedenborg describes comes, I think, after long self-observation. It is a lot for John to see that what he is saying is not just nasty, but a sin — a sin that is detrimental to his own Work and destructive to the people he is talking about. John's decision, "I will not do it," has to come from a strong emotional understanding that only follows his observation of the nature of what he is doing. The hells have John captive to something that is destructive. It is a lot for him to say, "I will not do it because it is a sin," if he has done no Work preceding it.

Genesis speaks of sin as "turning away." Doing something that the Lord forbids is turning away from God. The Work defines sin as "missing the mark." If in our Work we have set for ourselves an aim, from what the Lord has asked, anything contrary to that aim is sin. Simply put, if our goal is Philadelphia, but when we get to the Pike, we turn away from Philadelphia, we have sinned. If our aim is not to be mechanical, when we find ourselves talking mechanically about someone else's marriage, we are sinning against our aim to be conscious. It is very important in the evaluation of our Work to clarify our aim. The Writings tell us not to choose slander "because it is a sin." If John Doe decides that his judgment of Edgar and Sally comes from hell, he sees his words as sin, not as harmless happenstance.

We make a mistake when we think of the Commandments only in their external, or literal, sense, and assure ourselves that if we ever have the intention of breaking one, of committing adultery or stealing or killing, we will tell ourselves not to do so. We are an internal church, and we must recognize that there are internal meanings to the Commandments. Our intention reaches into our everyday conversation at parties and at the table over dinner. We need to see that the Work is to be done there, that the battle comes right into our life on that plane, that it is there that the internal becomes external. It is on the external plane that we must see that our slanderous talk comes from the other world and is injected from the hells into what we consider "only natural to talk about." That is exactly right — it is *natural*. It is external.

The battle is between the natural, external person and the spiritual, internal person. The external person must be made obedient to the internal person. We can do and say anything that is consistent with love of the neighbor, but not those things that are contrary to love of the Lord and love of the neighbor. Those contrary things are the natural external that must be tamed and made obedient to the spiritual internal. We read in *Arcana Celestia:*

> The work of regeneration is chiefly concerned in bringing about the correspondence of the natural man to the rational man, not only in general but also in particular. The natural man is reduced to correspondence by the Lord through the rational, and the good is insinuated into the rational; and in this good, as in ground, truths will be implanted, and then by means of the rational truths the natural man is to be reduced to obedience, and when it obeys, then it corresponds. And in so far as it corresponds, so far the man is regenerated. (3286[3])

> For man is regenerated as to his rational before he is regenerated as to his natural, because the natural is altogether in the world and in the natural as in a plain, there are found many thoughts in the will. This is why during regeneration man observes a combat going on between his rational or his internal man and his natural or his external man, and why his external man is regenerated so much later, and likewise, with much greater difficulty than his internal man. For that which is nearer to the world and nearer to the body cannot easily be constrained to render obedience to the internal man, but only after considerable length of time and by means of many new states into which the man is introduced, which are states of self-acknowledgment and acknowledgment of the Lord, that is, of one's own wretchedness and of the Lord's mercy. (3469)

Swedenborg paints a really clear picture of the combat that takes place between our natural person and our spiritual, internal person. Our rational is regenerated first by the Lord. We can understand truths, and love truths, and wish to live by them, long before we are *able* to live that way. Bringing our natural person into obedience to our spiritual person is our aim — and what the Work is all about — but the Writings tell us that it takes a long time. The coming of order requires us to acknowledge the wretchedness of the proprium. It requires us to see the damage done by the natural person, the proprium.

Almost everything on a sailboat moves: sails, pulleys, tiller, rudder. But the keel does not move. The keel keeps the boat from sliding across the water. The resistance of the keel allows us to steer the boat. In the Work, there are things that do not change and that act for us as a keel does for a boat. One of them is the uselessness of negative emotions. That does not change, although people new to the Work often want to argue about it. Certainly we feel that there are situations in which expressing a negative seems justified. But after some time in the Work, we see that there is absolutely no good reason to ever express negative emotions. That understanding acts as a keel, allowing us to keep our course. When we are on course, we see our justifications and rationalizations for what they are: excuses for the hells to live in us and for our identification with them. Not expressing negatives is a keel keeping us on course.

Another unchanging tenet is that we have no reason to dislike other people. Of course, our proprial mind, our formatory dialogue, doesn't agree. "There must be *some* people you shouldn't like," IT claims. From reading the newspaper, we know of rapists, arsonists and killers. Our proprium insists, "You can't reasonably like *them*."

We all have friends we like who have certain behaviors that we don't like. Maybe they drink too much or they smoke or they're a little obscene sometimes or they talk too much, but we still like them. When we are with them at a party, we may say, "You'd better watch it; you're acting a little bizarre tonight. Can't you calm down?" We don't pretend that their negative behavior doesn't exist, but we still love them. We like these people in spite of some poor behavior.

Do we feel the same way about the people whom we mechanically dislike? No, we just dislike them — it has nothing to do with their behavior. I mean here the people we meet in an ordinary day, the people we work with, or the people who walk into church, people who lead decent lives, not rapists, arsonists and killers. Dislike of such people is automatic and has little or nothing to do with their behavior. It is love of self in comparison with others, contempt for others in comparison with ourselves. Our understanding that such dislike is always an unquestionable sign that we should work serves us as a keel.

The proprium has apparently good reasons to dislike people. IT thinks that IT dislikes someone because of something IT knows about them. Maybe IT heard that someone actually voted Democratic, or IT heard that someone wanted a variance to build a house that IT did not want built. But what we find is that the proprium does not dislike people because of what IT knows; IT dislikes people because of what IT does not know, and there are myriad things that IT does not know.

For about fifteen years, I have been in the business of probation. Rapists, arsonists and killers are my clients. The more I get to know them, the more I like them all. Once I heard on the radio that a man had sexually abused an Avon lady. I immediately hated that guy. It really disgusted me. When I saw it on T.V., I had the same reaction — I hated him. But eventually, I was assigned to do a presentence report on him. I was glad, because now I could actually put my contempt on a face and do my hating in person.

I knocked on the door of his house, and there he was, an old guy in a wheelchair. He had been disabled for twenty years. The only people he saw each day were volunteers from Meals on Wheels. Between their visits, he watched T.V. That was his whole life, Meals on Wheels and T.V. — until the friendly Avon lady rang his bell. He felt that he just had to have a date with her. The more I learned about him, including the abuse he had suffered as a child, the more I liked him. I did recommend that he go to jail. He had definitely committed a crime. But I liked him. In the cases I handle, people have done some despicable things, but the more I get to know about them, the more I like them.

I have had other experiences of disliking someone I did not know, then coming to know them and liking them very much. When I was in school, a new boy moved into town. I detested that kid. I knew nothing about him and had never even talked to him, but he was a good athlete and I thought he was conceited. Eventually, we were forced onto the same team, and I came to love the guy. In fact, he became one of my best friends. The proprium can instantly dislike someone for the least of reasons. IT can dislike a stranger because she wears a raincoat with a rip in it. The proprium figures that is sufficient information upon which to base ITs dislike. One of our keels in the Work is that there is no reason to dislike another person.

Sensing can be another keel. When I am inundated with the hells and IT is screaming at me the reasons why this time IT is right, I try to develop the strongest sensation possible in my hand. If I put my energy into my hand instead of into reaction to my negative feelings, I see things that I do not see otherwise. At least one part of me is acknowledging that it is time to Work, even though I may be totally incapable of Work at that time. Sensing may sound like a strange thing to do, but it helps. It is a practice of self-remembering, and we are told time and again in the Work to remember and observe ourselves.

One day, we will get a strong negative emotion, but because we have practiced, we will put our energy into self-remembering and something will happen and our state will change. It will no longer be just theoretical. The day will come when we will say, "I don't want to Work, but I'm going to Work anyway, because the Lord wants me to." And we will Work. That Work may not help at once, but sooner or later, our state will change because we have done the Work. It will no longer be theory.

Let's do a short visualization in which we depend upon our subconscious mind to give us answers that can neutralize the mechanical dislikes that our proprium promotes all day long:

Let us now relax and permit our subconscious to bring to mind whatever it wants. There is no success or failure to this — whatever comes to mind is fine. If the image of a rabbit is suggested, but the image of an elephant comes to mind instead, that is fine. We will pay attention to whatever comes up. We will permit our right brain to do all the work for us as we relax. Now we may be able to recall someone we know whom we believe does not like us because of something they think they know about us, something they heard about us, perhaps something about our political, religious or social views, or how we raise our family, or do our work, or some habit or characteristic we have.

Let us hold the image of the person who doesn't like us, but let our hurt and unpleasant feelings fade away, so we see just the person, without the hurt involved. Now let us become aware of the difference between what they think they know about us and what they don't know about us, what they do not *understand* about our life. What a big difference that is, how very large. There are so many things that they could never know or guess about the many sides of our complex life. Let us be aware of the many, many things that we could tell them about us that they do not know.

Now we can let those thoughts and images fade away, as a hot-air balloon moves higher and higher until it is only a tiny speck in the sky, and bring to mind the image of someone whom we dislike because of something we know about them, something we know without perhaps even knowing *how* we know it. Let us become aware of what it is we know about them, and of how much we might *not* know about them. Now, in our imagination, let us permit that person to tell us the many things about them that we do not know. As we listen, we may experience a change in our feelings, a lessening of our dislike. The things they tell us may begin to lessen the disparity between what we know about them and what they know about their own life. This visualization leads to our present task.

The task concerns our proprium's dislike of people. We will observe our dislike of someone. Then we will estimate how much we know about them as a percentage of how much there is to know about them. If we dislike someone because she wears a torn raincoat, what percentage of all there is to know about her does her torn raincoat amount to? If she's married, perhaps her husband knows things about her that we do not. If she has friends, perhaps they see in her things that we have not yet seen. If she has children who are affectionate toward her, maybe she has attributes of which we are unaware. Her husband and her children and her friends may be total idiots, but maybe they are not.

How much information does our proprium need before it is willing to dislike someone, in comparison with what there is to know? In the task, we may find that despite thinking that we dislike people because of what we know about them, we actually dislike them because of all the things we don't know! In doing the task, we are free simply to make up all sorts of wonderful things about the person we dislike to see if we can come to like them. This is easy to do, and our subconscious won't know the difference.

The fact is that IT dislikes everyone, including our best friends. That perverse truth is one way to identify IT as our proprium. When we hear that something unfortunate happened to a friend whom we like, and we experience a feeling of pleasure at the news, a little shiver of delight, we are witnessing IT in action. We love our friends and are dismayed at their misfortune, but our proprium is glad. Likewise, if a friend hits the lottery jackpot, the part of us that resents that news is our proprium. IT is more than happy to come between us and our friends and families, even to seeing those relationships destroyed.

We cannot change IT. We cannot turn the active proprium away from ITs evil designs. But we can separate from IT. We can refuse to believe what IT says. We can decline to take the delight that IT offers. ITs existence is no cause for shame. Things are just the way they are, and although we cannot do, we must do what we can, as Nicoll suggests in *Commentaries*:

> Suppose you realize that something is a weakness and that you must struggle with it, but you find you do not have enough energy. You could then try to do something smaller, which is not so difficult and in this way save energy. Generally speaking, we miss the opportunity of making small efforts. We disregard them, do not consider them important enough, yet we can increase our capacity for making efforts only by making these small efforts which we often disregard. Before you can reach your remote aims there are many things you can do here and now. Man is afraid to see himself but he can decide to take the courage to see what he really is.

We cannot change the proprium's dislike of people. But we can observe IT, in preparation for the day when we can totally ignore IT and act from love. Our task gives us practice in that observation.

THE TASK:

To observe our dislike of someone, and to estimate, as a fraction of all there is to know about that person, the amount of knowledge upon which our dislike is based.

Entering the
Upper Room

There I was, watching T.V. and listening to my bath run upstairs. I was thinking how nice it was going to be to get into a hot bath before I went out on the cold porch to go to sleep. I got up and got ready to get into the bath. I put my hand under the faucet to check the water temperature. It was cold!

I was furious! I thought, "I can't believe it — every time I want to take a bath, someone runs the dishwasher and uses all the hot water!" Then I remembered the Work. I managed to remember not to express negative emotions. That was about as far as I was able to go in the Work. I resisted asking my family, "Did you run the dishwasher?" with just the proper intonation to let everyone know I was really irritated. I tried to resist really slamming the bathroom door, but nevertheless did slam it a little harder than usual. I tried to get ready for a cold bath, thinking, "Boy, this is going to be tough." Finally, I stepped into the tub. The water was hot! It was just the way I like it. It had just started to run cold when I put my hand under the faucet.

As I was sitting in my nice hot bath, I thought, "Well, it certainly wasn't cold water that made me angry, because the water is hot. If it wasn't cold water, what did make me angry?" Of course, it was the thought that the water was cold. It was my desire for hot water and my perception of interference with that desire that produced my anger.

One way to assess our level of being is to notice the things that we attract, the things that recur in our life. If I am one who wants to get places fast, I drive very fast, and anyone driving slower appears to be causing my impatience. I may not realize that it is my impatience that causes me to drive fast and that causes my life to be about everyone else going slow. It looks to me like slow drivers are causing my impatience, just as it looked like cold water was causing my anger. Our level of being attracts our life. Which negative states recur in our life? They have little to do with "the way life is." They have a whole lot to do with our level of being, the level of being of our proprium.

Our friends often know our level of being, but we seldom know it ourselves. If we ask our good friends what they know about us, objectively, and if we are capable of listening, we may discover something about our level of being. We have buffers and false personality and other things we use to hide from ourselves, but we do not generally hide from our friends, although they are usually kind enough not to bring our faults up unless we ask. Even then, they sometimes are not willing to tell us everything because they like to remain our friends.

The Work also confirms that we enjoy an objectivity concerning the level of being of others that we do not possess about our own level of being, as Nicoll notes in *Commentaries:*

> In the Work sense, observing "I" is the result of this Work and its ideas. We no longer observe ourselves from the life point of view, but from the Work point of view, and if we do this sincerely, even for a short time, we can no longer remain satisfied with our present level of being. Now if anyone takes himself or herself in hand in the Work sense, they must isolate themselves from the influences of life, and begin to follow the influences of the Work, or doctrine. A person in the Work must begin to resist the influences of life.

With respect to my bath, I could certainly say that it is natural to expect a hot bath and to be upset when I find it cold. It is also natural to blame someone. After all, it is frequently true that someone has run the dishwasher just before I want hot water. So what is the problem with my natural irritation and anger?

One problem is the negativity itself. I need to let go of the experience of being angry. Another very bad thing is that IT wants to communicate ITSELF to others. Telling someone I am angry creates distance between us. All negative emotions separate us from people. Thus, unless we separate ourselves from our natural, recurring daily irritations, we will experience separation from our loved ones. There is no irritation so small that the effort to elevate ourselves in order to come closer to others is not worth it. There actually can be love of the neighbor. We separate ourselves from life influences by seeing that they are not as innocent as we suppose, in that we pay a very high price for our "natural" reactions. Nicoll continues on this theme:

> Try to see for yourself by direct observation how negative states drain force from you. And try to see what happens when, having observed your condition, you genuinely try to separate from this state. If you do this rightly, you will experience a sensation that you have suddenly escaped from something evil, something that you did not realize was evil.

> The great key to self-change lies in observing oneself; observing how one talks, what opinion one constantly repeats, what one constantly condemns in others, what one is so proud of, and so on. You cannot change otherwise, because if you take yourself for granted as always being right, you cannot change.

It is possible for us to enter into the upper room to which Jesus took the disciples by getting into our observing "I" and looking down on the proprium from what we understand from doctrine and revelation. Again, we read in Nicoll's *Commentaries*:

> In a way, you can, as it were, deduce your level of being from noticing what always happens to you, because your level of being attracts your life.

> We must all practice inner silence toward one another, stopping inner talk in regard to objecting to one another. If we stop all this mechanical objecting, we begin to include other people in our life.

And, in Ouspensky's *The Fourth Way*:

> We think it is very easy to change something, but it is only when we sincerely try that we realize how difficult it is, how almost impossible it is. The idea of change of being is the most important idea in this Work, for if we want to change something in our own understanding of the world, we must, of course, change something in our-

selves.

The first step toward non-identification, of course, is self-observation. One must watch all impressions the moment they come in. An emotion that cannot become negative gives enormous understanding. It has enormous cognitive value. It connects things that cannot be connected in ordinary states.

Who has ears to hear can hear many changes of voice. Every center, every part of a center, every part of a part of a center, has a different voice, but few people have ears to hear them. For those who can hear it, it is easy to distinguish many things. For instance, if you speak the truth, it is one voice. If you lie, it is another voice. If you base things on imagination, yet another. It is quite unmistakable.

In *The Spiritual Diary*, Swedenborg writes that everything is revealed in sound. The sound of our voice reveals the nature of our affections. If we listen, we may discover when we are lying just by the variance in our voice. If we learn the sound of lying in our voice, it is a great tool of self-discovery.

The Writings teach that one scruple will block a thousand confirmations, just as one grain of sand can block the entire universe. We often insist that there are some things that justify anger and dislike. Hitler, for instance. By making exceptions of these justified angers, we neglect Working on many angers that interfere with our relationships. This is the result of our negative doubt, which leads us not to believe fully in the Work until it is proven to us in its entirety.

Zeal is an example of this. Of course, there is negative zeal, from an evil love, and positive zeal, from a good love. The zeal of an evil love attacks, the zeal of a good love defends. Externally, they appear the same. Internally, they are entirely different. If we pay attention to our internal thoughts and feelings, we will not mistake our anger for zeal. They will appear to us entirely different from each other, and we will no longer be unwilling to let go of our anger because we think it might be justified as zeal. Is our attitude toward our justified angers one of the scruples that blocks a thousand confirmations? Swedenborg writes in Arcana Celestia:

Spiritual indignation, and still more celestial indignation, derives nothing from anger, but it is from the
internal essence of zeal, which zeal in the external form
appears like anger, but in the internal form is not even
indignation of anger but it is a sadness with a prayerful
wish that it not be so. He who is in anger intends evil to
the others, but he who is in zeal intends good to him
towards whom he has zeal. The zeal of a good love is
like a heavenly flame which never bursts forth against
another, but only defends itself. The zeal of a good love
instantly burns out and becomes mild as soon as the
assailant ceases the attack. The good have no wrath or
anger, but only zeal. In the external form it appears like
anger, but inwardly is nothing but charity, goodness,
and forbearance. Anger belongs to those who are in the
love of self and love of the world, but zeal to those who
are in love of the Lord and love towards the neighbor,
so that zeal has regard to the salvation of man, and
anger to the condemnation of man. (3909e)

We have mentioned that the Work advises us to remember ourselves once a day, and if we can't remember ourselves once a day,
then to remember ourselves three times a day. What is it to remember ourselves? The Work uses a little story to describe
remembering ourselves:

A drama company wanted to really understand the play they
were producing in the coming year. They decided that they needed
to go somewhere they could all be together to concentrate on their
parts. They wanted to get into their roles to the degree that they
could feel what it would be like to actually be the characters in the
play. They found an island on which there were hotels and restau-
rants, and they rented the entire island for the whole summer.

Some were cast as queens, some as kings, some as dukes, some
were servants, some soldiers, and some were slaves. Their plan was
successful. On the island, they became better and better at playing
their parts, really getting into their roles. But they didn't notice
that, although they had arrived on the island as friends, now there
were groups that did not really associate with one another. The
kings, queens and dukes were mostly spending their time with each
other, while the servants and slaves were hanging out together elsewhere. After a while, they walked on different sides of the street.

Eventually, they would have nothing to do with each other.

Toward the end of the summer, a friend arrived on the island to visit an actor who was playing a king. The visitor asked about their mutual friend, Harry, another actor in the company.

The king replied, "I don't see much of Harry."

The visitor said, "Really? I thought you two were best friends!"

"Well, yes, but Harry's a slave," the king replied.

"Harry's not a slave," the visitor exclaimed. "In fact, he's a Rockefeller! He's just *playing* a slave. He's not a real slave, any more than you're a real king! Don't you remember?"

Self-remembering is the realization that we think we are our hereditary role. However, although letting go of our false personality is part of self-remembering, it is by no means all that self-remembering can be. What we remember is that this is just the natural world we are in. Everything that our senses take in from "out there" is the natural world. As wonderful as this world is, the only true reality is in the spiritual world. We remember that we are spiritual beings. We remember that everything we see in the natural world is a manifestation of spiritual forces. We remember that our spirit is in the spiritual world right now. Our moods, our thoughts, our feelings — our natural realities — come from the spiritual world. We can enter into that spiritual world, rather than immersing ourselves in the things of the natural world while forgetting what is possible. Not only may we enter into the courtyard of our spiritual house, we can go to the upper room in that house.

My proprial anger at my cold bathwater arises on a very low level. But self-remembering is not simply my *knowledge* of that. It is the will to separate from my proprium in that moment of negativity. That requires effort and attention and emotional intensity. My knowledge that there are spiritual forces acting in my life puts me in the courtyard of my spiritual house. To enter into the upper room of that house requires of me a determination to remember my spirituality and its purpose.

In the external plane, a single action looks very simple. In reality, everything is wonderfully complex. If I move a piece of paper from one place to another, it appears to be a simple matter. But is it really simple? No. Even considering it only in its physiological aspects, we find that it is extremely complex. My thought to move the paper, the conversion of that thought to a neural signal, the transfer of that signal by neurons to the muscles of my arm and hand, my capacity to use the proper tongue positions to vocalize what I am doing, these things are miraculously complex.

If we consider the spiritual aspects of my action, which society my thought to move the paper comes from, which affections in the spiritual world are involved in the communication of my thought, we are amazed at all that is going on in our life. In the natural plane, we lose touch with how magnificent and totally inexplicable this miracle is. We don't get it. We forget.

To help us to remember, to help us to get it, we can read what God has said to us through Emanuel Swedenborg. This is not psychological theory. It is not Freud's description of what he *thinks* goes on. This is God, explaining what does go on. We know that this is true because God is talking here about internals, of which we could not possibly know anything unless God felt it was worth telling us. Reading these excerpts from *Arcana Celestia* will probably take about four minutes, which, by the way, Gurdjieff said was twice as long as it is possible for anyone to remember themselves:

> The influx from the spiritual world into man is, in general, of such a nature that man cannot think or will anything of himself but everything flows in. For there is only one life, that is the Lord's which flows into all, but is variously received, and indeed, according to the quality which a man has induced on his soul by his very life. (5846)

> In order to know the interiors of a man, it is necessary to know that there is an internal man and an external man, and that the internal man is in the spiritual world, and that the external man is in the natural world. In man the spiritual world is conjoined with the natural world, consequently, that with him the spiritual world flows into the natural world in such a vivid manner that he can notice it, provided that he starts to pay attention. (6057)

> Evil spirits put on, especially, man's persuasions and cupidities and when they put them on they rule the man despotically, for he who induces man into his cupidities and into his persuasions, subjects the man to himself and makes him his servant, whereas influx from angels

takes place in accord with man's affections which they gently lead and bend to good, and do not break, the very influx being tacit and scarcely perceptible, for it flows into man's interiors. (6205)

Man is said to think in the sensuous, but when he thinks interiorly he is said to be withdrawn from things of the senses. That man can be withdrawn from things of the senses was known to the ancients and therefore, also, some of them have written about this state. (6201)

In the case of a man who is in the natural desire and delight of the love of self, and of the world, and regards these as his end, diabolical spirits are so near him as to be in him and to rule both his thoughts and his affections. The deceitful, who appear directly above the head, have occasionally flowed into me with such subtlety that I knew not whence the influx was, and also, that I scarcely perceived otherwise than that what flowed in was in myself and from myself, as is usual with others, but as I knew of certainty that it was from another source, perception was given me by the Lord so exquisite that I perceived each single influx from them, also where they were and who they were. When they observed this, they were very indignant, especially because I reflected upon what came from them; this reflection flowed in through angels. (3842)

It has sometimes happened that I was earnestly thinking about worldly things and about such things as give great concern to most people, mainly, about possessions, acquirement of riches and pleasures, and so forth. At these times I noticed that I was sinking down into what was sensuous and that in proportion as my thought was immersed in such things, I was removed from the company of angels. (6210)

That "sinking down" is exactly what it is to fall asleep, to forget. We all have seen parents at a mall, scolding their toddler, "I told you to watch that ice cream." Or, "Watch out! You're making a mess! Can't you ever pay attention?" They have forgotten their love for their child. However, if they are distracted momentarily and when they look again, their child is not there, they suddenly remember! It would be useful for them to remember that love when they're about ready to smack the kid for spilling ice cream. But to remember that there is affection and love involved, not just neatly eating an ice cream cone, takes effort and the determination to separate.

Remembering ourselves once a day is an effort to get in touch with higher influences, to elevate ourselves, to get the emotional impact of what's going on. Sometimes that happens unintentionally: while a couple is fighting, the husband has a heart attack. Whatever the argument was about disappears as the wife remembers how much she loves him. But to volitionally remember during a negative state that the Lord wants love to flow through us to others is self-remembering, and that self-remembering allows our state to change.

Recalling the myriad complexities in my simple act of moving a piece of paper, we may note that the technique of holography has demonstrated that every part of something contains the whole. That assertion has been made since ancient times, but holography allowed science to demonstrate that it is true. Swedenborg says that every thought, every affection, contains the entire person, that every sound of the voice tells everything about the whole person. It is interesting that holography now demonstrates the macrocosm and the microcosm. *Arcana Celestia* shows that we are each a heaven in ourselves:

> Every affection, although it appears simple and as one thing, nevertheless contains things within it so innumerable that it cannot be comprehended, still less described, for in every affection there is the person's whole life that has been acquired from infancy even to the time of life when he is in the affection; nay, there are even other things besides. That such is the case appears incredible to us, and yet it is true. (3078)

An exercise in the Work involves contemplating an object in an effort to realize all the things that are connected to it. Such an object could be a lamp. What went into the production of the lamp? We notice that the lamp is brass and contains wire, materials that had to be mined. The mining required tools. The tools were conceived by an inventor. If the inventor came to America from England in a steamship, shipwrights are implicit. Besides the shipwrights, someone had to discover the steam engine. Before long, we realize that everything in the universe is necessary for this lamp to be here before us right now. Nothing is omitted. That is the thrust of what holography reveals. And that is what the Writings tell us: everything is reflected everywhere in everything.

12

THE "BRING YOUR OWN" CLASS

Following the presentation of the material in Chapter 11, I asked the Aim participants to "bring their own class" to our next session. I asked that each of them come prepared to share for a few minutes something meaningful to their spiritual growth — a reading, or an experience, or a meditation or visualization. This chapter is the result of that request. The first experience shared concerned applying the Work to negative emotions.

"Our family discovered that one of us had a serious medical problem that might require various drastic measures. This time was full of negative emotions for me. By observing myself and remembering the Work, much of the time I was able to control them. The twenty-third Psalm was very helpful in restoring my trust in Providence, and to my understanding that the Lord is always looking to eternity and trying to lift things toward good. By myself, I am unable to see past my nose. So I spent time saying the twenty-third Psalm and reflecting on Divine Providence, very conscious of the Work during the whole weekend, and it worked, because I really was able to stay relatively calm about it and not go crazy.

"In contrast to that, yesterday we called the doctor at eight-thirty in the morning. He wasn't in, so we left a message for him, but he didn't call back. When we called again, the doctor was busy, and my Work-'I' went out the window. All the negative emotions I could possibly think of came up. Not only was I imagining the worst, I was also thinking nasty things about the doctor, whom I had never met. I could see the contrast between my two states, but I couldn't stop this one. I went to my job, but couldn't concentrate on anything. I spent my time pacing up and down.

"Looking back on those different states, I can see that being able to stop thought and prevent those negative emotions from controlling me is a lot better than worrying. And it turned out that a lot of what I was fearing was a big lie. All the horrible things I was worried about are not going to happen. It was a good Work experience, if not a good experience."

"You could see," I commented, "a lot of the things that the Work talks about: identification, nonidentification, imagination, and changing the level of our thoughts. Strong states like that allow us to see the Work in a way that we don't in normal states."

"I remembered the advice that we should practice on little things, and I was glad that I had had an opportunity to practice before on things that didn't matter as much to me as this did. This mattered to me!"

"It was like having practiced swimming in a baby pool. When you fell into the ocean in a storm, you were more prepared."

The next person shared about an inspiration from the Word.

"In the Book of Jonah, I read the story of Jonah's disobedience when the Lord told him to do something. Jonah decided instead to make up his own doctrine. He felt very superior and didn't want to go to Nineveh. Reading that story gave me a good feeling about how the Lord protects us even when we are stubborn."

"The Lord protected Jonah throughout," I added, "allowing him to go through trouble, but at the same time lifting him up."

"Yes. Throughout the Old Testament, people are doing horrible things, but the Lord is constantly saving them."

Another person conceived and wrote a visualization for the class.

"While we are becoming comfortable, let us hear a tale that some say is true. As our eyes gently close, we may notice our breathing slowing to a restful pace, letting us relax in a pleasant state. Our minds may have thoughts, but we can be calm and simply let those thoughts pass through like clouds drifting by on a summer's day, while we go together to a far away time and place.

"In a lily pond, the leaves of the water lilies look like emeralds, big, green, beautiful emeralds, shining in the sunlight. The worm-like family of insects known as Odonatas lives in the pond, clinging to the lily stems and bunched in the shade of the cool water under the lily pads. The sun cannot be seen from there, although, when it is still, some sunlight does filter down through the water. The Odonatas' round little bodies cling desperately to the stems, for they can't swim well, and if they let go of the lilies, the current will carry them toward the muddy shore, and who knows what might happen to them there?

"Life in the lily pond is very lazy and uneventful, except when a storm comes and tosses things about, or a big fish swims by. Then, the Odonatas huddle together in terror until the danger passes on. And, once in a great while, they catch sight of a flying creature high above them. This beautiful, winged creature sometimes flies low over the lily pads, but when that happens, even though the creature is very beautiful, the Odonatas hide their heads, cover their little ears, and tremble — just in case of danger. Soon, the hovering creature rises again, straight into the air, and flies off into the blue sky as swiftly as the wind.

"The elder Odonatas say that in the long, long ago, the Maker told their ancestors that a great gift awaited them in the lands beyond the pond, if they had the courage to seek it. But few of the Odonatas had dared to go, and none had ever returned. 'Who among them has come back to us?' the Odonatas would sadly ask. 'Not one. Not one,' was the answer. So life beyond the lily pond remained a mystery filled with fear.

"But in spring, the young nymphs of the family would talk of daring to go on the great quest. They spoke in low voices of the pictures they saw in their imaginations, of excitement, danger and adventure. They thought of the brave deeds they would do to seek the Maker's gift, and of the longing in their hearts to know another way of life in a land strange to their parents and to them. Finally, fired by these dreams, five nymphs made a plan, determined to make the trip toward the unknown. They made a raft of braided reeds with lily pads atop it, and collected strong sticks to paddle with, and prayed to the Maker for a safe, swift journey.

"Early one morning, with much anticipation and suspense, they sailed off upon their quest. They trembled as they let go of the sturdy lily stems to climb aboard the raft. Then, as they waved goodbye, a stiff breeze sprang up and carried them quickly out onto the swell and soon they were far from home.

"Back among the lily pads, the days and then the weeks went slowly by. The Odonatas felt hope ebbing from their hearts. They looked at the shaded spots where the nymphs used to play and their spirits sank. They fell to wondering...wondering...wondering.

"Meanwhile, the brave little crew had indeed found adventure on the ripples of the pond! Sailing in the sunshine was a very pleasant new experience, but a storm came up that nearly drowned them when the raft was overturned by the strong north wind not once, but twice. One day, a very big fish put his nose under the raft and tumbled it over. Fortunately, a huge turtle distracted the fish and the nymphs were able to climb aboard again. The trip was long and there were other dangers to survive. Seven weeks passed before careful maneuvering brought them close to land. But finally, with a bump and a lurch, the raft and riders were thrown upon the shore. Dazed and exhausted, the nymphs lay close together in the soft, warm mud at the edge of the pond. As fireflies turned their tiny lanterns on and off in the gathering dusk, the weary nymphs at last took their well-earned rest.

"Awakening late the next morning, they looked about wide-eyed at strange new sights: trees with luscious fruit hanging from their boughs, birds of bright colors, butterflies of every possible description, and timid rabbits peering from beneath berry bushes. The Odonatas rubbed their eyes, crawled out of the warm mud where they had slept so long, and basked in the golden morning sunshine. They felt their skins loosen and, slowly, they shed their skins for the very last time. One by one they emerged, to their surprise and delight each a stunning dragonfly!

"Two found that they had bodies of blue, while two were brown and one was green. Each lovely dragonfly had four gossamer wings that gleamed and glistened with cascading reflections of iridescent rainbows from the sunlight all about them. Lifting their new wings, they found to their amazement that they could actually fly! And fly they did, high above the land, fast and slow, far and wide, beholding the wonders of the world and of the heavens. In freedom, they soared among the clouds, dipping, swirling, rising again, their lilting movements a joyful sky-dance of love and gratitude to the Maker for this gift of flight beyond their hopes. Thus did the dragonflies take to the sky, pausing to listen to the rush of a waterfall below, feeling their wings brushing lightly, in passing, the leaves of a tree, looking down on a fawn standing still in a forest clearing, watching laughing children wade and splash in a stream.

"Sometimes, they flew over the lily pond, but never landed, since their delicate legs were not made for landing. But they could hover above the Odonatas' home and hope to be heard. Their lovely wings shimmered and fluttered in the soft air, and their hearts beat fast with eagerness to share the news of their joyous gift. Hovering gently above the lily pads, they tried with every cell of their being to convey to those below that the Maker's promised gift was great indeed. Then they flew off into the blue sky until another day.

"Now it is time for us, too, to leave the lily pond until another day, to come back to the present, taking whatever time we need to return to this room, feeling rested and alert, refreshed and renewed, ready to be here and enjoy the rest of our class together. When we are ready, we may open our eyes and really BE HERE."

I thought that visualization was beautiful. When it ended, I felt like I was in a trance. Another class member shared about the difficulty of sharing.

"I don't really have anything prepared. There have been huge things going on and I have been completely involved with the family this week. Anyway, I have found presenting things to a group a problem for years."

"Do you feel any separation from it, or do you feel very close to it?"

"Some separation. It is something the Lord has helped me with over the years. I can look back and see that it has improved somewhat."

"So you can see that the Lord is still working on your relationship to all that."

Someone else talked about a sermon from the previous week.

"The sermon was about the New Church as a state in which we see the Lord transfigured inside ourselves. There is the angry God of the Old Testament, then the state of the Christian church, in which we are invited halfway up the mountain to be with the Lord. The New-Church state occurs when we allow the Lord to come into our life and experience the Lord inside us. Working on our negatives, trying to see the negatives with clarity, allows us to move up the mountain (although the sermon never actually said that). I saw it as something I would like to do, and I knew it would be a new experience. It isn't really clear to me what it would be like to see the Lord shining through the negative and to see and experience who I really am, and who we all really are, but I feel that it would be very life-changing."

"For me," I responded, "stopping thought is like that, and it is very powerful. Wilson Van Dusen talks about the appearance that we have egos that are separate from each other, whereas there is really only one living voice in the room, and that voice is coming through each speaker. The Lord's one and only living voice is in what each of us has to say, from the same light. The Work has the capacity to bring people together in the experience of expressing the same life, whereas the hells divide and separate and individualize. There is no competition in the Work, which does away with better and worse, removing barriers so that there is no separation or effort to make oneself better or different than others. There is only one life. It is all the Lord's. And the awareness of the Lord is in all of us."

One member of our class shared readings that were of particular personal significance for her.

"I have been thinking how neat it is to bring our own class, because there is no way to do it wrong! My own is my own and can't be someone else's. That helps me to bring my own, because I want to share the stuff from the Work that has been the most powerful to me. This particular paragraph from Nicoll's *Commentaries* has just made a huge difference for me:

> The Work says you have a right not to be negative. As was pointed out, it does not say you have no right to be negative. If you will think of the difference, you will see how great it is. To feel that you have a right not to be negative means you are well on your way to real inner work on yourself in regard to negative states. To be able to feel this draws down force to help you. You stand upright, as it were, in yourself, among all the mess of your negativity and you feel and know that it is not necessary to lie down in that mess. To say this phrase the right way to yourself, to feel the meaning of the words, "I have a right not to be negative," is actually a form of self-remembering, feeling a trace of real "I" that lifts you up above the level of your negative "I's," which are always telling you without a pause that you have every right to be negative. Every negative "I" has only one purpose, to get a hold on you, and feed upon you, and strengthen itself at your expense. The real cause of negative states is in yourself, in negative "I's" that live only to persuade you with their half-truths and lies and to rule over you and spoil your lives. All negative "I's" only wish to destroy you, to ruin your lives.

The part in which Nicoll describes the lower and higher levels in us has also been very meaningful to me:

> The Work is to make us live on a higher level of our-
> selves and asks, "If you are in a negative state, are you
> in a higher or lower level of yourself?" You are on the
> lower level and you will not be able to taste what a
> higher level is like as long as you indulge unchecked in
> your negative states.

And here are passages from the *Arcana* on the same subject:

> The truths of faith which have been inrooted by means
> of the affection of truth, are the plane into which angels
> work, wherefore they who have not this plane, cannot
> be led by angels but suffer themselves to be led by hell,
> for the working of the angels can not then be fixed any-
> where but flows through. But this plane cannot be
> acquired unless the truths of faith have been put into act
> and thus implanted in the will and through the will in
> the life. It is also worthy of mention that the working of
> the angels into those truths of faith with man, seldom
> takes place manifestly, that is so as to excite thought
> about this truth. (5893)

> But in order that the angels may be able to avert the
> influxes from hell, there must be in the man truths of
> faith joined to good of life, into which they may flow.
> These must be the plane into which they operate. But if
> a man have no such things, he is carried away by hell.
> (5854)

> Be it further known, that all evil flows in from hell and
> all good through heaven from the Lord, but the reason
> why evil is appropriated to man is that he believes and
> persuades himself that he thinks and does it from him-
> self, and in this way makes it his own. If he believed as is
> really the case, then evil would not be appropriated to
> him, but good from the Lord would be appropriated to
> him, for the moment that evil flowed in, he would
> reflect that it was from the evil spirits with him and as
> soon as he thought this, the angels would avert and
> reject it, for the influx of the angels is into what a man

knows and believes, but not into what a man does not know and does not believe. (6206)

"Those things together have just been crucial to me. The part about the angels being able to flow into the truth that we know and have tried to apply seems to me real connected to the Work. That I am not my negative thoughts and that I need to separate from them, that negative thoughts are always counter-productive and bad for me, these seem like truths that the angels can flow into to help me deal with the stuff that is coming from the hells. It was just stunning to me when I first realized the power of that: that if I don't have a truth that I can think of, the angels really can't do much for me at that moment. The Work has given me truths to hang onto in those crucial moments of being tested, and they create that higher plane where the angels can work and help me. It seems to me that the idea that we have the right not to be negative is expressed in the Writings, too.

"I would also like to say that I, too, had the experience that my husband described earlier, of being able to stop thought and not fall into all my negative imaginings during the week of our family medical crisis. But when my expectation that the doctor would act in a certain way was disappointed, it absolutely knocked all the rest of it right out the window. I really got to experience that we cannot do, and neither can I! When the doctor finally did call, I was so upset that I couldn't talk to him. I had gotten myself so upset with worry about what might or might not happen that I could hardly feel relieved when we actually got good news. I realized that observing alone is not enough, even though it is better than nothing."

"It is a start," I replied. "I used to think that when my expectations about a doctor were disappointed and my negative emotions overtook me, I had failed. But from the Writings, I now more clearly understand that the Lord allows me down into my proprium to let me see the contrast between my states. Unless the Lord gives me this experience, I really can't see the quality of the state I was in, so that one state really is being used to demonstrate the nature of another state. There is no failure involved. The Lord knew what was going to happen to you in the state you were in.

"You can get value from looking back on both those states. A lot of value may come from looking at being identified with your proprium. If you had been able to stay in that positive state throughout your experience, you may have missed something the Lord wanted you to see. We don't attribute failure to ourselves any more than we attribute to ourselves our ability not to identify with evil. Neither of those is from us. We are only the vessel. The experience of both of those states is given to us in order that we may use them to raise ourselves to a higher level. The temptation to feel guilt at our failure is the other side of the temptation to feel merit at our success, and it really takes away from what we can get from our experience.

"I want to follow up what was said before about angels flowing into the truths that we have applied in our life, which is when we are getting truth from good. That can be related to the natural experience of effort. In coaching a diver, there comes a point when it must be said, 'I have told you everything about the possibility of doing this particular dive. But because you have never done it, I cannot talk to you anymore until you try it.' When the diver asks if the experience will be successful, the answer is, 'Probably not, but there is nothing I can put into your experience through words because you haven't had the experience yet.'

"Talk can only bring us to a certain point. Then we must make the effort to do the dive, or whatever task is before us in our life. Our first dive is probably sloppy, so we try again. But now our coach can talk to us from our experience. Before our effort, the truth of the dive had no place to rest, just as the angels had no place to put their help before we applied some truths to our life. The truth has to refer to some experience. That is why our tasks and our efforts to use our Work-'I's' are so important. When we have made the effort, we can really talk about something. That change in mind, by means of the experience of truth, is very powerful. In regard to that, Swedenborg writes in *True Christian Religion*:

> All the evils to which man is prone by birth, are inscribed on the will of his natural man, and these, so far as he draws upon them, flow into his thoughts. Similarly, goods and truths from above from the Lord, also flow into his thoughts, and are there poised like weights on a scale or a balance. If man then adopts evil, it is received by his old will and added to its store, but if he adopts good and truth, the Lord then forms a new will and a new understanding, above the old. There the

> Lord successively implants new goods, by means of truths, and by means of these, he slowly subdues the evils which are beneath, and he removes them and reduces all of these things to order. From this it is evident that the thought has a purifying and purging effect upon one's hereditary evil. (659)

It is in our 'thinking from goods' that the Lord operates to subdue and order what is below in the natural person.

"For my part of class, I brought a story from *King Arthur and His Noble Knights*.. Sir Lancelot is doing Work. At a certain point in the Work, Lancelot turns to face the source of all real battles — that source is, of course, within himself.

"Here is the context in which this takes place: Lancelot has brought peace to Camelot. Yet now the younger knights are secretly laughing at Lancelot and his contemporaries. They no longer believe the stories of glory the older knights tell — they think such tales are a joke. And it is true that many of the older knights may have forgotten how to fight: their armor is getting rusty and they are getting chubby, for there is no longer any big evil to fight against.

"However, the kingdom is full of petty squabbles. The knights decide that, by turns, one older and one younger knight will ride together through the kingdom as The King's Peace and attempt to settle these disputes. The first pairing is Sir Lancelot, the best knight, with his nephew, Lionel, the kingdom's worst young man.

"Lionel doesn't want to go, since he thinks of Uncle Lance as a fuddy-duddy. But Lionel's young friends say to him, 'Just go with him, and while you're out there, ask him a bunch of personal questions. When you return, we'll have plenty of laughs making fun of him.' Lionel does just that. He starts by questioning Lancelot about his love for Queen Gwenivere. Lancelot graciously tries to explain chaste love. At one point, Lionel asks:

" 'Yeah, yeah, but are you content with just that? My Uncle, please don't be angry, it is the question of a young man. You love a lady, a lady who...'

" 'It is well known and no secret,' said Lancelot. 'I love the Queen and I will serve her all my days.'

" 'Sir, I mean no disrespect...' said Lionel.

" 'Well, see you do not then, or you will find your death in it, nephew or not.'

" 'Most perfect knight, by which is understood, perfect lover, does he never sigh, yearn, suffer, burn, desire to touch his love?'

" 'I will answer your question. To sigh for my lady's favor, yes. To yearn for her grace, again yes. To suffer when she is displeased, triple yes. But to burn, to desire? That is not knighthood. Could I love my Queen, who is wife to my liege King, and desire her without dishonoring all three of us? I hope you find your question answered.'

"For a time they rode in silence. Then, Sir Lionel said, 'I must ask it, even at risk of your displeasure, Sir.'

" 'Very well, what is your question? And let it be your last.'

" 'Are you content with it?'

"A black rage shook Sir Lancelot. He drew his lips back from his teeth in a snarl. His right hand flashed like a snake to his sword's hilt and half the silver blade slipped from its scabbard. Lionel felt the wind of a death blow against his cheek. But then, in this one man Lionel saw a combat more savage than ever he had seen between two. He saw wounds given and received, a heart riven to bursting, and, too, he saw victory: the death of rage, the sick triumph of Sir Lancelot, the sweat-ringed, fevered eyes hooded like a hawk's, the right arm lashed and muzzled, while the blade crept back into its kennel.

" 'Here is the end of the forest,' said Sir Lancelot. 'How lovely is the sun on the golden grass.'

"Then the world's greatest knight turned to Lionel, smiling. 'Tell them that I was sleepy. Tell them that I was sleepier than I had been in seven years. And tell your young friends that I looked for a little piece of shade to comfort me against the sun.'

"And Lionel knew how hard the fight had been, how tiring the victory. Sir Lancelot lay in the grass under an apple tree, his helmet for a pillow, and fell into the darkest of all caverns of forgetfulness. Sir Lionel sat beside his Uncle and knew that he had seen greatness beyond reason, and courage that made words seem craven, and peace that must be earned with agony. And Lionel felt small and mean and treacherous as a dung fly, while Sir Lancelot slept like carven alabaster.

"Watching over the sleeping knight, Sir Lionel thought of the endless talking of the young knights, gathered to celebrate death without having lived, critics of combat whose hands had never held a sword, losers who had laid no wager. He remembered how they said that this sleeping knight was too stupid to know that he was ridiculous and too innocent to see the life all around him. And in his ears, Lionel could hear the words of failure, weakness and poverty, sneering that victory, strength and riches are illusions.

"Sir Lionel knew that this sleeping knight would charge to his known defeat with neither hesitation nor despair, and finally would accept his death with courtesy and grace, as though it were a prize — and suddenly Sir Lionel knew why Lancelot would gallop down the centuries, spear at rest, gathering men's hearts on his lance like tilting rings. He chose his side, and it was Lancelot's. He brushed a fly from the sleeping face."

THE TASK:

To conduct an inner dialogue with a friend while we are experiencing a negative emotion, telling our friend how we are applying the Work to our negative state.

1 3

TRANQUIL
ANXIETY

In the Work, we look at our negative states with noncritical, nonjudgmental observation. But it is very difficult to objectively observe a negative state in ourselves without any criticism or guilt or emotional reaction going along with our observation. The Work likens it to turning on the light in a messy room. The light doesn't make any comment about the room, it just sheds light on the situation. We may see by means of the light that the room needs to be cleaned. But if we turn the light off because seeing the messy room makes us feel terrible, we aren't going to get a whole lot of effective cleaning done in the dark — our viewpoint will be subjective and we will lack the objective observation necessary to getting some real cleaning done. As Nicoll writes in *Commentaries*:

> How can you expect to have any degree of inner freedom if you are at the mercy of every change, every event, every little incident in your external life? If everything upsets you so easily, how can you have inner freedom?

So Swedenborg writes in *Arcana Celestia*:

> I have spoken with good spirits about the internal and the external man, saying that it is amazing that few within the church believe, although they know it from the Word, that there is an internal man distinct from the external, when yet they might know this from a slight daily inspection of their own thoughts and will. (6309)

> The order of influx is that evil spirits first flow in and then angels disperse that action. Man does not always perceive that there is such influx in him, because he does not attend to such things, nor could an evil man know even if he did attend, because with him there is no equilibrium between evil and good. But they who are in good can know it, and also that the spiritual man fights against the natural, thus the angels who are in the man's interiors and in spiritual things, fight against the evil spirits who are in his exteriors and in his natural things. (6308)

When we hear about good influx and bad influx, sometimes we want to immediately stop the bad influx. But we should just watch it for a while. I think that despair can be caused by our attempts to correct our evils too soon, before we know what is going on. Our objective observation is very productive, even though it appears that we are making no effort to change our bad states.

Our efforts to achieve objective observation are made more difficult because we have been taught by our parents and teachers from when we were in kindergarten that there is good and there is bad, that is, we have historical faith and derived doctrine. We have propriums with opinions about what is good and what is bad, and what should and should not be done. Getting back to objectivity from there can be very difficult.

But we also have true doctrine, and as we give up derived doctrine and historical faith, we go to the Word ourselves to gain true doctrine to bring to our incoming impressions. We observe our states. Perhaps we have reached the stage in which we can observe influx from hell through the proprium, or perhaps good influx from heaven through the new will. From our observation of influx, we do have some hints about what is good and what is bad. For instance, negative emotions like anger, frustration, covetousness, or any response that leaves us contemptuous of another, are influxes from hell into the proprium.

How loudly, how forcefully, do we experience our thoughts and emotions? Good spirits flowing into our internal person are nearly imperceptible. The Writings refer to their influx as silent thought, slight perceptions, a tender awareness. Good spirits are very gentle and very quiet, whereas the hells flow into our external person with a racket! The Writings note that influx from hell gives us the erroneous impression that evil is much stronger and more pervasive than good. Because we are in our external person and because that is where evil spirits attack us, we are unaware of the equilibrium the Lord provides for us.

Some evils are so widespread and common that they are familiar to all of us. We can see them in ourselves without many hints. Three such loves are those of honor, reputation and gain. The Writings often group them together, and for good reason, I think, but right now let's just consider love of reputation.

Let's imagine that we're in the bathtub, relaxing in the nice hot water, eyes closed, letting the heat soothe and please us. Now, without opening our eyes, let's imagine we're in our brand-new, six-thousand-dollar hot tub. Does it feel any different than the bath? Or, is there a different feeling if we imagine relaxing in the hot springs near our newly-purchased summer home overlooking the ocean? If there is a difference in the way we feel from the way we feel in the bathtub, what is the difference? In all our images, our eyes are closed, we are relaxed, we are experiencing the pleasing sensations of hot water. So what accounts for a difference?

We can imagine flying in an airliner, and we can imagine flying in our own brand-new Learjet. We can imagine driving a Volkswagen, and we can imagine driving a plush new Rolls-Royce. Do these images feel different to us? Is the difference attributable to our love of reputation?

If we hit the lottery for ten million dollars, won't we feel different tomorrow than we do today? What will happen? It's not likely that our level of being will change overnight, or the extent of our knowledge, but we will feel different. Is that different feeling our love of reputation? If we win, can we take our ticket to the state cashier, bring the money back home, put it in the bank and *never tell anyone?* Or, will we have the urge to tell someone, and does that urge arise from our love of reputation?

Suppose a friend tells us some very personal thing that we know we should not share with other people. But while talking with another friend, we reveal the personal thing we know. Later, remembering that our two friends often see each other, we become afraid that one will find out from the other that we have told. We enhanced our reputation by telling something that only we knew, but now our reputation is threatened if we are found out. To do the Work here, inner separation will be very important because these feelings are bound up with love of reputation, a very damaging emotion that works in a subtle way that we tend not to notice. It seems sort of okay, but it is not. We must notice it, observe it, and remember that love of reputation is IT.

Besides our awareness of negative states and their Influx into the proprium, we want to be aware of influx into the new will, or the new understanding. What is that influx like? We already know that good influx is very quiet. It is silent thought that is barely perceptible. It is lighter and softer than negative influx. Nicoll describes it:

> When the Work begins to enter a man more deeply, it sets up a continual conflict. Not a violent agitated conflict, but a quiet almost wordless conflict. All the time he is aware that there is something new in him that is always acting on him in a silent way without persuasion and without compulsion.

And Swedenborg writes of it in *Arcana Celestia*:

> Elevation from sensuous things was known to the ancients and therefore, when the lower mind is withdrawn from these sensuous things, their wise men said that they came into interior light and, at the same time, into a tranquil state. (6313)

Further light on influx into the new will is shed by The Blessings from the Sermon on the Mount, *Matthew* 5:3-10. In the course of our regeneration, when one state is full, we go into the next state. I think a similar transition is possible for us who are listening to the Lord, not only over time, but within our own present experience. We come to points at which we have a choice between one state and another, if we can perceive them both. For instance, when it is said, "Blessed are the meek," I think the Lord is saying that there is this quality in us that is blessed, if we listen to it, if we pay attention to it, if we look for it, if we are open to it. We might even notice these good qualities in ourselves during certain of our states. We talk about the different "I's" in us, including our Work-"I's." So there are different states in us. If we pay attention, we may notice that some of these states are blessed. Is the Lord describing blessed states that are available to us, within us, right now?

Blessed are the poor in spirit, for theirs is the kingdom of heaven.

Blessed are they that mourn, for they shall be comforted.

Blessed are the meek, for they shall inherit the earth.

Blessed are they who do hunger and thirst after righteousness, for they shall be filled.

Blessed are the merciful, for they shall obtain mercy.

Blessed are the pure in heart, for they shall see God.

Blessed are the peacemakers, for they shall be called the children of God.

I believe that these states reside within us, in the internal person into which the heavens flow. I believe that we can see them and know their nature: they are meek, they are humble, they are poor in spirit. They are not lovers of reputation, they are not rich in self.

Describing our internal and our external, Swedenborg, in *True Christian Religion*, compares a person to a three-story house:

Interior men are spiritual because they think from the spirit elevated above the body and therefore see truths in light. External men are sensual and natural beings because they think from the fallacies of the senses. Internal men are like those who stand on a mountain in a plain, or in a tower in a city, whereas external men are like those who stand in a valley at the foot of a mountain, or in a vault under a tower, who see nothing but what is very close to them. Moreover, internal men are like those who live in a second or third story of a house, or a palace, the walls of which have spacious windows of clear glass, who have an extensive view of the city in all directions and know every little building in it. External men are like those who live in the lowest story, the windows of which are made of paper pasted together, who do not see even a single street outside of the house, but only the things which are within. Lastly, internal men perceive that what they know, compared

to what they do not know, is like a pitcher of water
compared to the ocean, while external men fancy that
they know everything. (839)

I suggest that the entry into the third story, its gate or door, is
acceptance. The first thing I ever read that helped to lead me to the
Work was the phrase by Krishnamurti, "All anxiety is the nonacceptance of what is." I started working with that phrase in my life
and I noticed that it is true: if I can come to a total acceptance of
what is, it is a gateway to tranquillity.

On one level, acceptance of what is means accepting our lot,
accepting that we are short, or an accountant, or have no children.
But I think it means more than that. I think it means accepting
each moment as it is, which includes the state we are in.
Acceptance of each moment includes accepting the stage of regeneration we are in. We know that the Lord introduces us into
elevated states, and also allows us to drop down into proprial
states. Accepting both kinds of states is very important. If we can
accept, we can achieve tranquillity. If we can accept that we are
anxious, we can be tranquil. That is, although it sounds strange,
we can be anxious and tranquil at the same time.

How is such a dual state possible? It is possible, and only possible, if we use two different places within us: if, while our external
person in the first story is anxious, we put our feeling of "I," our
observing Work-"I," into that third-story room with our internal
person and observe from there the anxiety of our external person,
we can experience tranquillity. Our internal person is capable of
accepting the Lord's request that we experience our present stage
of regeneration, which may be frustration or anger or jealousy or
covetousness — or anxiety.

The Lord asks us to look at love of reputation. Can we look at
it from our internal person, accept it, and be tranquil? What does
that take? It takes inner separation, nonidentification, raising ourselves into the rational, and bringing the Work to our incoming
impressions. Let's consider two phrases that sound very similar,
but in fact are very different. They provide a good way to think
about what we have been discussing.

The first phrase is, "I am.........., and I shouldn't be." Fill in the
blank with any negative emotion: "I am angry, and I shouldn't
be," for instance, or "I am jealous, and I shouldn't be." The second phrase is, "IT is.........., but I don't have to be," as in, for

example, "IT is angry, but I don't have to be."

Now these are distinctly different statements. The first one, "I am angry, and I shouldn't be," signifies that we are in our external person, that IT is angry, that we are identified with IT, and that we are experiencing IT as ourselves, as "I." We know, somewhere in our brain, that the Lord says that it is not good to be angry, so we feel that we "shouldn't be" experiencing anger. But of course we *are* experiencing anger.

The second phrase, "IT is angry, but I don't have to be," signifies that we are in the third story of our house, observing that downstairs there may be stampeding rhinoceroses, wild tigers and warriors fighting with spears, but that we don't have to be down there, because "IT is angry, but I don't have to be."

When we believe that we do not have to be identified with ITs anger, we stand in a place of choice, as in a gateway, for implicit in our belief is the choice to experience anger if we *want* to. When the hells attack our external person, they are in their delight. In their attack, they offer their delight to us, and we can accept their offer to be angry. We can choose to be identified with the negative emotions in our external person or to rise above them by not identifying with them. We have a choice between the delights that the hells are offering to our external person and the tranquillity that comes with accepting whatever presently "is" in our life.

But we also can see clearly that our negative emotions are difficult to let go. We find that anger *does* offer us a certain delight and that we may actually want to be angry. We really *do* have a choice. There is no certainty that we will always prefer tranquillity. No, we are brought repeatedly to a point of real choice.

It is crucial to our tranquillity that we totally accept the way the proprium is. Suppose someone gets my name wrong, and calls me Paul rather than Peter. It is foolish to think that the proprium will not be angry when someone gets ITs name wrong, because IT loves ITs reputation and ITs honor. Of course IT is going to be upset. To feel that IT "shouldn't be" angry is foolish. If we left a group of two-year-olds in a room with jelly beans on the table and said, "Don't eat any, I'll be back in five minutes," what would we expect? Wouldn't it be foolish to expect them not to eat the jelly beans? The proprium will be the way the proprium will be. If we accept that IT behaves the way IT does, but that *we don't have to*, we gain some separation from IT in preparation for the time when our internal person is active enough that such behavior actually does not occur. But first of all we have to observe IT. Are we surprised at ITs behavior? Of course not — that is ITs nature.

The key is in our acceptance of that nature and our responses to attacks by the hells. In *Arcana Celestia*, Swedenborg writes:

> Persuasions originating in loves of self carry with them the desire to rule over all things, and in so far as the restraints placed upon them are loosened, they hasten to fulfill the desire, even to the extent of desiring to rule over the entire universe. But persuasions originating in love of the world do not go so far; they do not go beyond the insanity of not being satisfied with one's lot. (1675 [7])

Thus, through nonacceptance we enter insanity. God creates what is. When we do not accept what is, we live in insanity.

We need to remember that the *only* place at which the hells can attack us is our external person, and that if we are in our external, we will surely be attacked. But if we are capable of lifting our "I" out of identity with the proprium and into our internal, our third-story room, our sense of who we are is not available to the hells and we cannot be attacked by them. It is our external person that wrongly says, "I shouldn't feel this way." IT will feel the way IT does because IT is where the hells reside. But when we come to that point of choice, we must accept all that is in order to experience the tranquillity of our internal. Acceptance and tranquillity go hand in hand.

Thus, when we are in a negative state, we remind ourselves, "IT is.........., but I don't have to be." We focus on that reminder until we feel ourselves arrive at a real point of choice. Then we say, "I can have this present state of.........., or I can accept what is and have tranquillity."

THE TASK:

*While in a negative state, to say to ourselves:
"IT is..........., but I don't have to be. I can either
have this present state of..........., or I can accept
what is and have tranquillity."*

14

TOWARD A
HEAVENLY PROPRIUM

We are all familiar with the ad campaign, "Just say 'No' to drugs." Its advice to teenagers is to say 'No' to all drugs all the time. It advises an absolute 'No,' so that kids don't have to make distinctions among cocaine, opium, hashish, marijuana, heroin and speed. All drugs are bad. None offers any positive benefit to youngsters. Similarly, we can see that our internal dialogue has nothing to offer that is of any benefit to us. Do we just say 'No' to that dialogue? When we say 'No' to our internal dialogue, we say, "I don't believe what you say, and I'm not going to act from what you tell me — I hear you, but I am not listening to you."

We have discussed many ways in which our internal dialogue expresses negatives about other people, but we can see that it also expresses negatives about *us*. The internal dialogue that tells us, "You always make a mess of things," and, "You're so stupid," does not come from angels. Good spirits do not say nasty things about our neighbors or about us. We can learn to say 'No' to that dialogue, too.

A child who wakes up on a moonlit night full of shadows may see a monster in the closet and hide under the pillow or call out in fear. The child believes that the monster is real and is there in the closet. When we are older and we look across the room at night and see what resembles a monster, we recognize that it is really our robe hung over the door. We know it is not a monster and we roll over and go back to sleep. We just say 'No' to that illusion.

The assertions that our proprium makes are likewise illusions. The guy who cuts us off with his car is not stupid. He is not an idiot. He is not uncivilized. Those characterizations are all illusions that our proprium offers to us in ITs dialogue. That dialogue is just like the shadows on the robe hung over the door. Our inherited proprium projects all that stuff onto the other driver, just as a child projects a monster onto a robe. Our mind is being used by the hells, but we don't have to listen to IT, and we don't have to believe IT, because we know IT has nothing good to offer us. We can just say 'No.'

The Word addresses our transition from the proprium consumed with love of self to the new heavenly proprium. Several passages in *Matthew* relate to the Work we are doing to allow the Lord to effect a change in us:

> No man can serve two masters, for either he will hate the one and love the other, or else he will hold to the one and despise the other. You cannot serve God and mammon. Therefore, I say unto you, take no thought for your life; what you shall eat or what you shall drink; nor yet for your body; what you shall put on. Is not life more than meat, and the body more than raiment? But seek ye first the kingdom of God and his righteousness and all these things shall be added unto you. Take therefore no thought for the morrow, for the morrow shall take thought for the things of itself. Sufficient unto the day is the evil thereof. (6:24-25, 6:33-34)

> Beware of false prophets which come to you in sheep's clothing, but inwardly they are raving wolves. You shall know them by their fruits. Do men gather grapes of thorns or figs of thistles? (7:15)

> Then his Lord, after he had called him, said unto him, "Oh, you wicked servant, I forgave you all your debt because you desired me to; should you not also have compassion on your fellow servants, even as I have had pity on you?" So likewise shall my Heavenly Father do also unto you, if you from your heart do not everyone forgive his brother his trespasses. (18:32-35)

> So when evening was come, the Lord of the vineyard said to his steward, "Call the laborers and give them their hire, beginning from the last to the first." And when they came who had been hired about the eleventh

hour, they received every man a penny, but when the first came they supposed that they should have received more, and they likewise received every man a penny. And when they had received it they murmured against the good man of the house, saying, "These last have worked only one hour and you have made them equal to us which have borne the burden and the heat of the day." So the last shall be first and the first shall be last, for many are called but few are chosen. (20:8-12,16)

We each have an exterior state, an interior, or rational, state, and an inmost internal state. The exterior is our lower natural person, and the internal is our highest spiritual person. The rational is between them and able to look either way, toward the Lord in heaven and thus receive heavenly influx, or toward the earth and thus be caught in the cares of the world, its negative emotions and thoughts of the morrow. We can look toward God or toward mammon.

In our Work, if we alternately look upward and downward as we remember and observe ourselves, something brand new happens: our internal looks through the rational into the natural and sees the falsities and evils there. If our rational looks both up and down, our internal, where the Lord resides, looks through and purifies our external. The internal above, looking through the rational to the external below, sees not only evils, but also mere apparent good where we thought there was real good.

We are told to serve God, not mammon. To do that, we must remember ourselves. We must ask the Lord to purify our attitudes. We must refrain from seeking those things that only make our senses happy. We must subdue our senses to purify ourselves. We must allow within us the change from a self-centered proprium to a heavenly proprium. The Lord asks us to serve that end instead of our natural desires.

The "me, mine, I" feelings of the proprium absorbed in love of self are obvious when we watch a group of children with cake and ice cream — "Me first! I want the biggest piece! My turn!" The kids don't try to hide their feelings because they aren't as concerned as we are with love of reputation, honor and gain. But those emotions are in us, too. They are the "mammon" emotions, love of self and love of the world. The new heavenly proprium is cleansed of love of self. The "me, mine, I" feelings and the "it's not fair" feelings are made passive. It is our untransformed proprial state that says it is just not fair for the eleventh-hour laborers to be paid the same as the others, and for that part of us it is *not* fair. After all, it is the kid who gets a smaller piece of cake who brings up the issue of fairness.

When the Word tells us that we must die to be born again, that when someone sues us we must give them not only our cloak but our coat, that when someone compels us to go a mile we must go two, it is telling us things that are totally impossible for our selfish *self* to understand. What Jesus asks of us is impossible for the self concerned with "me, mine, I." We must give up our self-importance. We must come to abhor the self. We must die to the self. We must sacrifice the self.

The Word tells us to forgive our debts. But we cannot forgive a debt unless it is actually owed. We often find it easy to forgive "debts" that we really are not owed. When someone cuts in front of us in the movie line, our proprium feels wronged, so we are then in a position to forgive the debt we think we hold. But really we aren't owed anything. It's the same when we order in a restaurant, but three other parties that came in after us are served first — the restaurant wronged us, and that is the time we choose to forgive, although we hold no real debt.

On the other hand, forgiving our debts does not mean that we ignore events on the external plane. Forgiveness requires us to consider both the external and the internal. When someone runs into our car, we take care of business on the external plane, asking for the other driver's identification, calling the insurance company, and all of that. Forgiveness does not require us to be a doormat in worldly matters. What it does require is that we separate from our proprium's anger and contempt and send them back to the hellish state that is tempting us to yell, "You stupid sonofabitch!" Forgiveness requires us to give up that state totally. We must not act from our proprial external hells at the expense of our spiritual internal.

We forgive others when we just say 'No' to that internal dialogue that is not willing or thinking good toward the neighbor. And we forgive ourselves when we just say 'No' to all those internal thoughts and feelings that are not willing or thinking good toward us. Which thoughts and feelings are these? We shall know them by their fruits. We can become more sensitive to good thoughts and feelings toward our neighbor and ourselves by asking whether they open us to being more useful, to being closer to people, or whether they close us down. Good things do not come from bad feelings, and bad feelings do not come from angels. Angels attribute the best to everyone. We judge by the fruit. When a harangue of internal dialogue starts, we ask, "How will this affect my relationships? Will the feelings be good or will they be bad?" Swedenborg deals with these themes in *Arcana Celestia*:

> The interior man perceives what is going on in the external man, just as if someone were to tell of that activity. The interior or rational man is situated between the internal man and the external man. The internal man communicates with the external by means of the interior, rational man. Without the interior or rational man between them no communication from one to the other is possible. The interior man is called the rational man and because it is situated between the two, it communicates in one direction with the internal man where there is good itself and truth itself, and in the other with the exterior man where there is evil and falsity. By means of this communication with the internal man a person is able to think about celestial and spiritual things and to look upward, and by means of communication with the external man a person is able, also, to think about worldly and bodily things and look downward almost in the way animals do. The interior man between the internal man and the external is spiritual or celestial when looking upwards, but merely animal when looking downwards. (1702)

> Once the internal man perceives within the interior or rational man that the state of the external man has been taken captive, meaning that not genuine but apparent goods and truths have taken possession of it, from which goods and truths he fought against so many foes, the internal man flows in and restores all things to order and releases the external man from the things that infest it. (1707 [4])

> Indeed it is evil spirits who activate evils and falsities; unless they do so a person scarcely knows that they are evils and falsities, but once activated they are evident,

and the longer the conflict that is brought about by temptation persists, the more evident such evils and falsities become, till at length they are regarded with abhorrence. The more a person contracts an abhorrence of evils and falsities the more love the Lord instills for goods and truths. The greater that abhorrence of evils and falsities becomes, the less do evil spirits dare to approach, for they cannot stand the aversion to and abhorrence of the evils and falsities constituting their very life. (1740)

The Writings also tell us that when we think well of the neighbor, we are with good spirits, and with bad spirits when we think evil of the neighbor. When we feel anger and contempt for the person who jumps ahead of us in the movie line, we tend to react with contempt for everyone we see. They are too fat or too skinny or too rich or too poor or too slow or too fast. It really doesn't matter what they are, for there isn't a human being we look at that doesn't make us sick. We may not believe what our proprium is telling us, and we may not act on ITs feelings, but we find IT continues to react with disgust and anger. When the proprial affection called anger is activated, everything IT sees makes IT angry. However, when we are involved in the Work, we may find just the opposite, that everyone we see brings the light to us, and there is no one who doesn't make us happy.

Neither of these conditions is us. They are states we are given. The state we are in affects how the world looks, and whether we project a monster or an angel onto the robe that hangs on our closet door. The images we see in a Rorschach test reveal nothing about the ink blots, but tell much about us.

The task is to forgive our debts as soon as we are owed. To be owed can mean someone bumps into our car or steps in front of us in line or fails to appreciate something we do. We will call these events debts that we are owed. When such an event occurs, we will recall a debt for which we would like to be forgiven by the Lord, and we will hold these debts side by side, and we will notice how they look. That's all.

O, Lord, if you mark iniquity, who shall stand? If the Lord were keeping accounts, we would all be in bad shape. But the Lord forgives us continually. When we mark iniquity, we will check our account against one we wish the Lord to forgive us.

THE TASK:

(1) To forgive our debtors as soon as we are owed;

(2) To place a debt we wish the Lord to forgive side by side with one we hold, and observe them.

1 5

LEST WE BE
DELIVERED

The Work is about getting a new will so that we can actually experience loving our neighbor. So, too, the aim of the Writings is coming to love our neighbor instead of ourselves and the world. When we argue about doctrine, we lose sight of our goal of reaching a state of acceptance and of willing good to our neighbor without regard to doctrine. We read in *Arcana*:

> Examine, if you care to, any doctrinal teaching so that you may see what they are and what they are not. Do they not all have regard to charity, and so to faith that derives from this charity? The essence of charity is to will good to others, from oneself and from what is one's own. By itself doctrine does not constitute the external aspect of the church, still less the internal, nor, on the Lord's part is it the teachings that make one church distinct and separate from another, but its life in accord with its teachings. What else does doctrine do but to teach man the kind of people that they ought to be? If they were to make love to the Lord the chief thing, doctrinal difference would be no more than shades of opinion which truly Christian people would leave to each individual's conscience and in their hearts they would say that a person is truly Christian when he lives as a Christian. If this were so all the different churches would become one and all the disagreements which stemmed from doctrine alone would disappear. Indeed, the hatred that one man holds against another would be dispelled in an instant and the Lord's kingdom on earth

would come. (1798-1800)

To achieve a state of love to the neighbor, we must receive a new will from the Lord. But before God can give us a new will, we must know the nature of our old will in order that we may earnestly desire to have a new one. We need to understand the nature of our old will as it flows into our thoughts, our emotions, our affections, and our body, so that we can separate from it. Without that awareness, we cannot identify influx from the other world as from heaven or from hell. If we remain unaware in the love of self, we never will be satisfied and we cannot be happy. Love of self is never satisfied. No lottery jackpot is big enough to sate our proprial desires.

And our love of self is always colliding with the affections of others. I drive a lot in my job, and I enjoy very much the trees and streams of the rural countryside. Recently, I noticed an area marked by stakes with little red flags tied to them. A few weeks later, I passed that way again and saw newly-built condominiums. It really made me angry. Those condominiums ruined the view! They ruined the countryside! Many others agreed with my angry attitude, but that only gave me further reason to be angry.

One day, as I passed those condos, I decided to try external consideration. I asked myself, "Alright, who is getting happiness by means of these condominiums?" Well, certainly the guy who sold the land must feel good about it. The developer also must be pleased. I assume that the families who bought them are happy, as well as the laborers who built them. I got in touch with the affections of those people and experienced the condos from their point of view. I realized that the development was probably a good thing for them. My negative emotions began to dissipate. I still can't say I am happy about those condos, but my negativity now is balanced by something else.

Even good loves collide when we are in love of self. My son plays drums. I love him and, for his sake, I love his practicing the drums. But I love quiet, too. Those loves collide and I cannot have both at the same time. To the degree that I truly enjoy my son's enjoyment, I am happy when he practices. The happier we can be with another's happiness, the happier the Lord can make us.

Forgiveness is an essential attitude in being passive to our proprial loves. To the extent that others don't go along with our desires, our opinions, our likes and dislikes, we have negative feelings toward them. Along the path from love of self to love of the neighbor, the practice of forgiveness is an important giving-up of some of our own, a giving-up to those who owe us.

Separation from our old will also requires us to give up our simplistic concept of fairness. We most often equate fairness with equality, and when we do, life doesn't seem fair. Life is fair if both of us get an equal piece of the pie — that's fair. But we can see that none of us looks much like the others — we aren't the same size or the same shape. Nor do we have the same job or the same house. Thus our worldly affairs do not reflect our simplistic notion of fairness. In nature, as well, God never creates two things that match, so the idea that fairness implies equality is not borne out by creation. A bird might feel that it isn't really fair that it can't swim, but if we hold him under water, he'll get the idea soon enough. Likewise, if we throw a disgruntled fish up in the air, is flying going to make him happy?

Fairness is found in the capacity *each of us* has to be totally happy in the form in which we exist. No one can be happier than I can be in the form that the Lord gives me. That's true fairness. But we must be passive to our simplistic idea of fairness. Someone got a raise. So what? We can be happy. Someone hit the jackpot. Let it go. We can be totally happy. Someone has a bigger house. We couldn't be happier.

In our transition from love of self to love of the neighbor, the sooner we work on the evils we encounter in ourselves, the less severe will be our imprisonment by them, and the easier it will be for us to gain freedom. A passage in *Matthew* gives warning:

> Agree with your adversary quickly while you are on the road with him, lest your adversary deliver you to the judge, the judge deliver you to the officer, and you are thrown in prison. Assuredly I say unto you that you will by no means get out of there until you have paid the last farthing. (5:25)

The judge, the officer, and prison are progressive degrees of captivity to evil. The time to deal with evils is while they are still in the street, that is, in our mind. The outer part of our mind accommodates all kinds of thoughts and feelings, always changing and always moving, one leading to the next and that one breaking upon another. A desire must have an agreement in our understanding to become a permanent part of us, because we judge from appearances and because we ascribe to ourselves all thoughts and feelings, especially the evil ones. However, we are not the adversaries who continually rise up to accuse us. We can stand apart from what we are thinking and from what we are feeling. We can evaluate, we can judge, and we can reject. This judgment that stands apart is the source of a healthy mind. When we use it, we are well-minded. We are able to sort and to choose. Well-mindedness springs from the Lord working in our new will and in our new understanding.

Evil enters into the will by being kept in the thought by consent. The sign that we are letting something gain entrance into our will is keeping it in our thought. While we think about it, we let it stand at the door, engage it in conversation, flirt with it, argue with it. This in fact amounts to our consent. Once we consent to an evil, it enters our will. Our adversary delivers us to the judge. But we are free to send our thoughts and feelings back into the street. We are able to deal with our adversary while we are in the road with him.

We discussed just saying 'No' to our internal dialogue. How quickly do we say 'No?' I can always tell when my mother gets a call from a telephone solicitor because she suddenly just hangs up. But I stay on the line far longer than she. I hem and haw. I thank the caller. I apologize to the caller. I tolerate the call. Now, the chances of selling my mother something on the phone are virtually nil. But since I stay on the phone longer, I am much more likely to buy the product. How quickly we say 'No' to influx from hell into the proprium affects whether IT flows only into our body, inflows into our thinking process, or is allowed to flow deeper and enter our will.

How quickly we reject evil, of course, depends upon how quickly we can identify IT as a negative proprial emotion that we want to reject. If we have to think about IT, consult our feelings about IT, debate about IT, we are slowed down considerably. While we are making our judgments about IT, it is possible we are being delivered from the street to the judge. Debating with the hells is as foolish as holding a hand under scalding-hot water while debating whether it is really scalding. We have barely enough time to get our hand out of the water before serious damage is done. If the water is just plain hot, we may have more time, but we want to make our decision quickly enough that our adversary cannot deliver us to the judge. *Matthew* again:

Get thee behind me, Satan, for you savor not the things which are of God, but the things which are of men. Whosoever will come after me, let him deny himself and take up his cross and follow me, for whosoever will save his life shall lose it; but whosoever shall lose his life for my sake, and for the Gospel's sake, the same shall save it. (16:23-25)

Our first 'No' is our easiest 'No,' because there is no delight involved. The 'No' I gave when I stopped drinking had a different quality than the 'No' I might have given as a youngster before I ever had my first beer. Both the nondrinker and the recovered alcoholic who say 'No' to a drink are free on the street, but there is a difference between the one who has been in prison and is now out on parole, and the one who has never been delivered to the judge or imprisoned by the alcoholic influx. There are degrees of servitude in all of our compulsions. Smokers and overeaters experience the same range of servitude from street to judge to officer to prison, and back again, as alcoholics do.

A nondrinker may take three seconds to decline an offered drink, and that's it. But a recovered alcoholic who is on parole from that influx faces hells that intend to deliver her into deeper captivity than that from which she has escaped. Her freedom is far more conditional than the nondrinker's. If she has one drink, her capacity to say 'No' to a second will be diminished greatly while the intensity of her desire for a second drink will increase. We must assess differently the risk to freedom faced by these two people. The nondrinker's risk is measured on a short scale that in this instance may be no longer than three seconds. The alcoholic's risk must be measured on a long scale that stretches over years and takes into account the hells by which she has already been imprisoned.

But nondrinking young people who say, "Okay, I'll have one beer," may become alcoholics if they begin to use alcohol to induce sleep, then begin to drink in the morning, and so forth. When they have been delivered deep into imprisonment by that adversary, they find they really have to Work to climb back to freedom. They may find that they have to pay the last farthing.

The assertion made by compulsives, "I can quit anytime I want," is the same one made by all of us with respect to our anger, contempt, deceit, dominion, and covetousness. We make the same rationalizations and justifications, although more subtly than an alcoholic. When we succumb to the temptation to talk behind people's backs, we notice how difficult it is to stop, even after we have made the decision to stop. And we notice how frequently we relapse. We can see that we are not on the street, we are not fully free, in regard to our gossiping. We have been delivered to the judge or to the officer. Perhaps we have been thrown in prison.

The levels of our captivity are a metaphor of the Work. With respect to an evil, we are on the street when we know and feel that it is wrong and abhor it. A recovered alcoholic is back in the street in regard to alcohol. He knows that drinking for him is wrong, he feels it is wrong and he has an abhorrence of it. He rejects a drink as though it were scalding water.

We are before the judge when we know an evil is bad, but we harbor a certain delight with IT that we are tempted to indulge. An easy but clear example is a diet. We know cake is contrary to the aim of our diet, but we are tempted to have it anyway. If we are in the very presence of cake at our child's birthday party, then the hells are standing in the door of our will, and we rationalize and justify — "This child is my first-born, at her first birthday party! People will be disappointed, even affronted, if I do not eat a piece of cake." We are struggling: our will has been stimulated and wants ITs way, but our understanding is still in charge. Perhaps we do not give in, but the temptation has threatened our freedom more than if we had rejected the cake out of hand. We have been before the judge.

We are delivered to the officer, or even thrown into prison, when we are subservient to an evil, albeit unwillingly so. We still know and feel that IT is wrong. But we presently cannot resist IT. We are enslaved to evil. We are thrown even deeper into prison when we think and feel that IT is good, when we are convinced that our action is justified and we feel fine about it. We are then so deep in prison that we do not even know that we are captive. We like prison, and we don't want to leave it.

How do we escape from prison? How do we get back to the street? The first thing we need is right thinking, called repentance. A lot of the Work is about repentance. The purpose of doctrine is for us to learn, not only that anger is not justified, but that it is not we who are angry — the hells are angry within us and we are subservient to them. Before we can make any movement toward freedom, we have to see that those things we think are good are bad, those things we think are true are false, and those things we love from love of self are wrong.

We emerge from prison and come before the judge when we can use our understanding against our old will, when we experience temptation but do not succumb, when we feel the impulse but still say 'No.' Through long observation, we can see the nature of that to which we are subservient, how IT affects us, and the price we pay for IT. Rather than thinking that what IT offers us is good, we see that IT is the hells that are out to destroy us. When we are on the street, our identification of proprial influx is not a matter of thinking, but an intuition that we recognize as a sensation in our body. We recoil from evil, much as we jerk our hand out of scalding water. We don't have to think about it.

The Writings tells us that the hells can argue against us forever. To them, it is nothing. If we get into an argument with them, we have already lost. We cannot stay on the line with a phone solicitor — we must reject the sale faster than that. Thus we must be able to identify the negative proprial influxes that we want to reject. The task is to discern the means by which we identify influx that is not from heaven.

We can see that with regard to some evils, we are on the street. Suppose we have the opportunity to sexually abuse a child. If we are on the street, we instinctively want nothing to do with it. We reject it out of hand — just that fast! With other opportunities, our responses may not be quite so clear or quite so fast. We want to discern when we are in the street, when we are before the judge, and when we are in prison in relation to the temptations we face.

The task also includes discovering the meaning of *Arcana Celestia* 1820 on the nature of temptation. Some of it is very clear, but some of it is not. What does it mean to us? Here it is:

> [2] Since few people know what temptations really are, let a brief explanation of them be given here. Evil spirits never contend against any other things than those which a person loves, and the more intensely he loves them the more fiercely do these spirits contend. As soon as they detect even the smallest thing that a person loves, or get a scent, so to speak, of what is delightful or precious to him, they attack this instantly and try to destroy it and the whole person, since his life consists of his love. Nothing ever gives them more pleasure and delight than

to destroy a person. Those who are ill-disposed and deceitful worm their way into those very loves by flattering them and, in this way, they bring a person in among themselves, and once they have so brought him in they very soon try to destroy his loves, and so to slay that person.

[3] Nor are the attacks which they make solely those in which they reason against goods and truths, the making of such attacks being nothing to them, for if they were defeated a thousand times over they would carry on with them because their supply of reasoning against goods and truths can never be exhausted, rather, in their attacks they pervert goods and truths, setting them ablaze with a certain kind of evil desire and a persuasion, so that the person himself does not even know any other than that a similar desire and desire reign within him. At the same time they infuse those goods and truths with a delight which they seize from the delight which that person has in some other thing. In this way they in fact infest him most deceitfully, doing it so skillfully by leading him from one thing to another that if the Lord did not come to his aid that person would never know otherwise than it was indeed so.

They act in similar ways against the affections for truth that constitute a conscience. As soon as they become aware of anything whatever the nature of it, that is constituent part of that conscience, they mold an affection out of the falsities and weakness that exist with that person, and by means of that affection they dim the light of truth and pervert it. Or else they cause him anxiety and torment. In addition to this, they keep his thought firmly fixed on one single thing and they fill that thought with delusions, at the same time secretly incorporating evil desires within those delusions.

What the hells do is very deceitful, very skillful, and if it weren't for the Lord's help, it would be hopeless for us. I am reminded of Reverend Jim Jones. Perhaps he began with real loves of his religion and of teaching others. The hells somehow flattered those loves, and then somehow brought in something else and inflamed it, until Jim Jones was persuading people to commit suicide. That was a very big change. How did it occur?

The task is to observe the signs of influx into the proprium. When we are happy, we recognize that we are happy because we hold an experience of happiness in our body. How do we know that we are having an evil thought? Do we feel it? Do we perceive it? Do we think about it? Do we debate about it? Do we reason about it? And how long does it take us to know it is an evil thought?

Whatever our experience with the task may be, we can see that when we are on the street, we must be able to say 'No' real fast. We must discover as soon as possible that we are getting a call we do not want, because the phone solicitor is a top-notch salesperson and we need to hang up right away, lest we be delivered.

THE TASK:

(1) To discern the means by which we identify influx not from heaven;

(2) To discover what Arcana Celestia 1820 means to us.

16

FROM KNOWLEDGE
TO EXPERIENCE

The Lord wants us to know and be with God. Yet we are permitted to decline that experience if we so choose. The Lord values our freedom above all. But if we choose to know and be with God, what do we need to do? We need to separate from the love of self. Innocence and wisdom then can flow into us and bring us into the awareness of God's presence. In *Heaven and Hell*, Swedenborg writes:

> In heaven the primary reason why angels are able to receive such great wisdom is namely that they are without the love of self; for to the extent that anyone is without the love of self, he can become wise. It is that love of self which closes up the interiors against the Lord and heaven. (272)

> One may learn what innocence is for it shines forth from the face of children. It can be seen that children have no internal thought, consequently, they have no prudence from their proprium, no purpose or deliberation, thus no intention of any evil nature. They are content with the few insignificant things presented to them and delight in them, they have no anxiety about food or clothing and none about the future, they do not look to the world or covet things. They suffer themselves to be led, they give heed and obey. (277)

> It is said in heaven that innocence dwells in wisdom and that an angel has as much wisdom as he has innocence.

This is confirmed by the fact that those who are in a state of innocence attribute nothing of good to themselves but regard all things as received and attribute them to the Lord, also, that they wish to be led by Him and not by themselves. Neither are they anxious about the future. Anxiety about the future, they call care for the morrow. As they who are in a state of innocence love nothing more than to be led by the Lord, attributing everything to Him, they are removed from their own proprium, and to the extent that they are removed from their own proprium, the Lord inflows. In consequence of this, whatever they hear from the Lord, whether through the Word or by means of preaching, they do not store it up in their memory but instantly obey it, that is, they will it, and do it, their will being itself their memory. (278)

The same is true of everyone who is being regenerated. Regeneration, as regards the spiritual man is a rebirth. As man advances in age goods and truths are given him by the Lord. At first he is led into knowledge of them, then from knowledge into intelligence, and finally from intelligence into wisdom, always accompanied by innocence, which consists, as has been said, in his knowing nothing of truth and being able to do nothing of good from himself, but only from the Lord. Without this faith and a perception of it, no one can receive anything of heaven. Therein does the innocence of heaven consist. (279)

There is pervasive change in one who is going from knowledge to intelligence, from intelligence to wisdom, from truth to good, from understanding a thing to the willing of it in actual experience. This change is always centered on a state of innocence and willingness to be led.

We are discussing that change from knowledge to experience, although in a sense it cannot be described, just as the taste of a mango or the sound of a symphony cannot be described. Talking about it is not the experience. But we know that a change from knowledge to experience does take place, for we all learned how to ride a bicycle. When we were applying what we had observed and been told about riding a bike, the front wheel wouldn't stop wobbling and we were constantly uncertain whether we were doing it all properly. At some point, however, the bicycle started to ride us. Then we were no longer in charge, and the doing of it was teaching us how to ride. We had made the change from knowledge to experience.

We know from the Gospel that we do not learn our way into heaven. Remember the young man who asked the Lord, "I have obeyed all the commandments since my youth — what else must I do?" The Lord answered, "Sell everything you have." The young man went away, sorrowful. We know that we must give up pride in our own intelligence and all the things we know, for it is harder for us to enter heaven rich with our own knowledge than it is for a camel to go through the eye of a needle.

There is the innocence of wisdom, which is internal, and the innocence of ignorance, which is external. A child has the innocence of ignorance, but is not without perception. If we blow smoke in the face of a five-year-old, the child knows that smoke is not good. That childhood innocence knows truth. But over time we lie to ourselves. We build up associations — we see someone we like smoking, and we talk ourselves into a lie, and eventually come to believe it. To experience the truth that the child does, we must surrender something we believe to be true, give up what we have come to feel is *us*.

But heaven is always available. Influx is always available. As we give up our proprial states, the Lord's presence becomes immediately available. When we give up impatience, we experience patience. When we give up covetousness, we experience contentment with what we have. We cannot remain the same and change, and we cannot change and remain the same. When we give up love of self, we experience loving others. The change is the experience of *allowing* loving others to occur. This is not easy. When we first give up impatience, we feel as though we have given up something that was right and that we were justified in having. The self-observation we do in the Work teaches us about our negative states and leads us toward the point at which we are willing to actually *allow* the experience of patience.

We protest that merely *allowing* something to occur is no more than idly waiting for influx — it's not *doing* anything. Not. It is doing a great deal. Who works harder, the piano student struggling to learn how to play, or the polished pianist? The struggling student works harder, but who is doing more *piano playing*? The accomplished pianist makes it look easy, and it is easy — there is nothing easier than the piece the pianist is playing. But it took twenty years for it to become that easy. In order to play well, the pianist at some point had to give up working at it, and *allow* it to be easy. That is the change from knowledge to experience.

On the other hand, the student who has not yet learned the skills, but decides to become a piano player just by "letting it all flow out," isn't an artist, either. We are not talking here of skipping over knowledge and just getting in touch with love. We cannot love our neighbor without any skill, or truth, to offer with affection. All the Work is important, including the lesser states in which we find ourselves at different stages of the Work, but at a certain point we must let go of knowing and thinking about our skills and allow the experience of the Lord's presence. It is a version of the truth that we cannot push our way into regeneration through effort. We cannot learn our way into regeneration. We can learn truths, but we must allow the Lord to regenerate us. And that is an *experience*.

The hells want us to think that heaven comes after we die. But the Lord tells us that the kingdom of heaven is within us. We make a mistake when we wait for heaven, wait for regeneration, wait for change. It is not going to happen in the future. It *is* happening. It is within our experience. Now is the time. We are here to do it, right now. Now is the first possibility of experiencing what truth is about. Truth is not about truth; truth is about good. It is the passage to new experience.

Right now is our experience. Right here. Right now. If we choose, we can experience our experience thinking about how nice it will be when we retire, or when it's Friday rather than Monday. But all we are ever going to experience is the experience we experience when we experience it. Be here now.

In one sense, there is no time. If we start a stopwatch so we can see the tenths of each second whipping by, we still can't say when *now* is. We can tell from the watch what was, but we can't stop in now. We can talk only about the past or about the future because *now* does not stop; it just keeps going. The same is true of space. Where do we think we are? Yes, we are on the earth. But the earth turns, so we are never in the same space, ever. And when we consider that the galaxy also turns, we realize that we are never *here* long enough to describe it! We can talk about where we have been and where we are going to be, but we can never really describe where we *are* because it is changing as we talk! Thus we are only going to have the experience we are experiencing when we are experiencing it.

How do we want our experience to be? Early one morning while on a walk, I sat by a river under a railroad bridge. I watched two men fishing off the bridge. It was an education. There was a river of difference between those two men. The first was shaking his rod and seemed anxious and impatient that the fish weren't biting. All of a sudden, it seemed like a fish was on his line, but it was just weeds. He struck his forehead with his hand as though he were angry.

The second man held his rod very lightly and seemed relaxed. I could see no hurry in his stance and he seemed to be aware. When a fish hit his line, he didn't get excited and grab it right away. He let the line run out a bit, for two, maybe three bites, then very purposefully set his reel and started to bring the fish in. But the fish spit the hook out and the line got all tangled up. The man went at it patiently, taking his time to unravel the mess. He seemed interested in it, like a puzzle. It took him ten minutes to tie a brand new knot, but he did it well and seemed pleased with it.

As I watched, I imagined that he had shaved carefully that morning, had a nice breakfast, taken time to sharpen his fillet knife, and gone fishing for the day. He seemed to enjoy the sun coming up, the birds, and the fresh morning air. Catching a fish was just one of the things that might happen in the course of his day. It seemed to me that the other man was there to catch a fish and nothing else, and I imagined that he hadn't shaved too well and may have nicked himself. On the way out the door, he may have said, "I'd like breakfast, but I better get on my way. I want the best spot on the bridge." I imagined that he hadn't sharpened his knife, and had forgotten some of his favorite lures.

When we are fully present with all five senses in the now, we do not feel that we *will* be happy when we catch a fish. Instead, we continually experience the now we are having, which includes the sunrise and a tangled line. When we fill our mind with anticipation of the future moment when we might catch a fish, we shut out a lot of our experience, and if the experience we're anticipating doesn't happen, we are real upset. There is a big difference between going fishing and setting out to catch a fish.

We are spiritual beings. The experience we want most from the

Work is to love the Lord with all our heart, and with all our mind, and with all our soul, and to love our neighbor as ourselves. That is not just knowledge. It is experience that we feel in our body. To love our neighbor as ourselves, we must give up our love of self by allowing the Lord to take it from us when we are ready. It is allowing truth to become wisdom, allowing knowledge to become experience, allowing the Lord to lead us. That is the aim of all the Work.

In The *Worship and Love of God*, Swedenborg writes poetically about God's creation of us as beings who can look into heaven and understand, and from that understanding look toward the earth, and see the conjunction between the two:

> But there was still wanting a being who could refer these pleasures of the senses to a sort of proper mind, or to his own consciousness and perception, and who, from the faculty of intellect, might decide upon the beauty resulting from all these harmonies, and might also from beauties perceive joys; from joys, grounded in a true origin, might form conclusions concerning goodness; and, lastly, from goodness might comprehend the nature of blessedness; there was wanting, I say, that son of the earth, or that mind under a human form, which from the paradise of earth might look into the paradise of heaven, and from this again into that of earth, and thus from a kind of interior sight embrace and measure both together, and from the conjunction of both be made sensible of pleasures to the full; consequently, who, from a kind of genuine fountain of gladness and of love, could venerate, and adore above everything, the Bestower and Creator of all things. There was no object, not even the least, from which some resemblance of Deity did not shine forth, and consequently none that was not desirous of offering itself to the enjoyment of such a being as could offer immortal thanks to that Deity for himself and for everything. (30)

This was written during the time that Swedenborg was having the dreams recorded in *Journal of Dreams*. The theory of Wilson Van Dusen is that Swedenborg then was in transition from a man of knowledge to a man of wisdom who experienced love and worship of the Lord. Swedenborg was, we might say, shifting from his left brain to his right brain, going from understanding to will.

In the same volume, Swedenborg describes how the will, or love, gave birth to two daughters called intelligences. The will, their mother, speaks to the intelligences, her daughters, about the relationship between the will and the understanding:

> The intelligences so intensely loved their mother that with difficulty they suffered themselves to be plucked from her embrace, and although removed, they still remained in her view, that they might obtain by sight what they could not secure by grasp, for love is an affection or union and in its purest state is such that one sees oneself altogether in another, separated indeed in nature, but not in mind. They were also made sensible in themselves of joy resulting from their gladness, but as yet they knew not that they were joys, conceding them only to be pure gladness, but afterwards when they became more intelligent, they began to think and to perceive that gladness and joy flowed from love as from a fountain, yea, they also saw clearly from their light that the truth, goodness, and joy had continual reference to love and was from love, wherefore they sought nothing more ardently than to embrace that love; thus they began to look at love as the end, and all other things as a means leading to it. On perceiving these things, the pious mother exalting as it were with gladness began to take the highest delight in her infants, as in an image of herself because from desire they both willed and regarded ends and between her kisses she saluted them no longer as intelligences but as wisdoms.

> She fixed her gaze upon each of them. She thus began to speak, "My most beloved daughters! the time is at hand that we must depart, you to your Socrates and I into my sanctuary. Remember, little daughters, that I am your parent and that the life which you derive from mine is so devoted to you by love itself, that by mind I am in you, thus although we part, still, you can do nothing but under my auspices. The light by which you view ends, is from mine, because by me; yours is to be circumspect, and to arrange means, that our ends may exist in effect and use.

"I have adorned you, not only with understanding but with will, and thus I have subjected my ends to your decision, but again and again I pray and beseech you, not to look at and covet any other end than the best, that is, the love of the Supreme, breathed into you with life and with milk, for He is the End of Ends, the First of the Last, and the Last of the First: from Him are all things because He is the All in All, hence your happiness and its joy; from your love you are loved and from His love you love, hence the light of your intuitions and the sacred warmth of your actions, for the rays of His light are so many truths and the fires of his rays are so many goodnesses. For the sake of His and your love, I abdicate my kingdom. Now I deliver up the key to you for care, for my great concern is only about you. Behold me, therefore, no longer as your lawful mother but as your companion and minister. But I entreat you, my most beloved and most dear, with the most earnest prayer. Remember my salvation, while you remember your own, for my salvation and happiness are at your disposal since I have delivered up to you my very soul." At these words tears flowed from the mother and her daughters; they sank into each other's bosoms and remained in close embrace. (48-49)

That is what is going on between our will and our understanding, and between the Lord and us. We can have that joy if we choose.

THE TASK:

*To choose someone whom we mechanically dis-
like, and to do the Work to consider that person
our friend.*

Glossary

from The Work

Aim: The object or end that one strives to attain.

Essence: The core, concentrated, indispensable God-given quality that make us what we are.

Esoteric: Intended only for people with special knowledge or interest; profound, deep, arcane, as in esoteric literature.

External consideration: Putting oneself in the neighbor's place and seeing from that point of view. Going out of oneself to consider the neighbor from their real or imagined experience. To see oneself in another, or find another in oneself. Also, to recall a time when we did the same or a similar thing as the neighbor.

False cause: Thinking an external event or situation is the cause of a state in oneself or others. All causes are internal.

Formatory mind: Natural, shallow, ritualistic manner of thinking; rote pattern-response. The formatory mind thinks in terms of black and white, yes and no.

Identification: Thinking and feeling that our thoughts and emotions are ourselves, instead of realizing they are influx from spirits and angels.

Internal consideration: Keeping count or "making accounts" in our mind of what we feel the neighbor owes us. Not forgiving imagined insults and slights.

Internal dialogue: The negative chatter we hear going on in our head without effort or attention.

IT: The proprium; hereditary inclination to evils of every kind.

Nonidentification: Not identifying with a state. Remaining conscious of the fact that the state with us is not us ; realizing, believing, and acknowledging that the thoughts we think and the feelings we feel are not us, but are of spirits or societies with us.

Observing "I": A part of us within which the new will can be born. A noncritical, nonjudgmental, observing part which can look down on our behavior; the rational.

Self-observation: Observing the behavior of the proprium, noticing what it thinks, says, and does. Looking impartially at one's own behavior from the observing "I," or the rational.

Self-remembering: Being here and aware of impressions coming into us and our responses to them — and then being aware of ourselves being aware of that. Also, feeling the Lord's presence with us — the "I AM" — knowing that only God lives.. "In God we live and breathe and have our being." Remembering the aim, end, or purpose of our existence.

Sensing: Putting attention on one place in our body until we can feel sensation there, and sustaining it during a negative state. Sensing is used to divide our attention from the incoming hells during a negative state. It reminds us, "Now is the time I will to Work."

The Work: One's inner, spiritual work; spiritual growth; the work of regeneration.

FROM THE WRITINGS

Angel: A person in heaven. In the Writings, all angels are people who lived in the natural world and entered heaven upon death.

Appearance: That which seems real to the natural eye or natural mind, but is actually illusion. It is an appearance that the sun rises and sets. The reality is that it is constant. It is an appearance that the Lord sometimes forsakes us. The reality is that God is always with us.

Appropriate: Taking and using as one's own; taking credit or blame for something. When we believe we are the source of good or evil, we wrongly appropriate it to ourselves and take on states of pride or guilt. All good is from heaven and all evil from hell.

As of self: The ability given to man by God to act entirely as if by his own power, while acknowledging that all power to do is from God alone. The "as of self" principle also acknowledges principle of the Work that we cannot do, but we must do what we can.

Conscience: Being with knowledge. Knowledge received from Revelation is taken into the understanding and becomes a perception of what is and what is not to be done. Conscience is acting in accord with the teachings of one's religion, after first acquiring those teachings. Conscience is therefore "built up" in one.

Corporeal: Bodily, physical.

Derived doctrine: Doctrine drawn, or asserted to be drawn, from true doctrine or revelation.

Doctrine: Religious teaching; religious principle.

Dominion: Rule over; control; domination.

Exterior person: The part of a person's mind that is relatively exterior or external, concerned primarily with the outer, material world, the self, honor, reputation, and gain. It contrasts with the interior person, which is concerned with higher, finer, more spiritual things. The exterior person reasons from appearances in the world, while the interior person reasons from the truth of revelation.

Historical faith: Faith based only on tradition, or on the beliefs of others.

Influx: That which flows in from spirits of heaven or hell. Higher or lower influences; heavenly or hellish influences.

Internal: The deepest spiritual part of a person; soul.

Love of self: Loving one's self only and not loving others except for selfish advantage; selfishness. (Note: there is also a good love of self, which is self-care and self-preservation, so as to be more useful to others.)

Love of the world: Preoccupation with success in worldly ambitions. The proper order is for us to love heavenly, spiritual things more than earthly, material things.

Love of the Lord: Believing and loving to do what the Lord teaches. "If you love Me, keep My commandments."

Love of the neighbor: Seeing good in all people; willing well to the neighbor; putting the best interpretation on the neighbor's actions; excusing with all our might.

Passive: Receptive; able to be acted upon. We are created that we may be passive recipients of the Lord's love, but in order to be so, we must actively resist evil.

Proprium: That which is our own. Hereditary inclination to evils of every kind. Selfish desires, preoccupation with self and the world rather than the neighbor and heaven. (Note: there is also a "heavenly proprium," which is gradually built up in us as we freely choose to withdraw from our selfish, hellish proprium.)

Rational: Reasoning level of the mind; reasoning ability.

Real "I": Spiritual essence; potential new will.

Regenerate: To spiritually renew; recreate, transform.

Regeneration: Lifelong process of spiritual rebirth.

Revelation: That which God has revealed and which we could not discover by ourselves.

Ruling love: The strongest love in one, which dominates one's life, thus the dominant love.

Understanding: Intellect; ability to understand, especially truth and falsity, and to distinguish between good and evil.

Will: Ability to love, feel, desire. We are born with our own will, a desire to love ourselves above others. Gradually, the Lord can build up in us a new will, a desire to love others as ourselves, and the Lord above all things.

Word: The Word of God; the scriptures as the Word of God.

Writings: The collected theological works of Emanuel Swedenborg.

About the Publisher

During the first half of the 19th century, an itinerant nurseryman named John Chapman criss-crossed thousands of miles planting apple orchards from the Ohio River to the Great Lakes. His unique worldly activity together with a singularly spiritual personality gave genesis to the legends of Johnny Appleseed. The spiritual inspiration for his life's work came to him through his less well-known cargo: the writing of Emanuel Swedenborg. Along with his apple seeds, he deposited Swedenborg books throughout the Midwest for forty years. Sometimes, when his inventory ran low, Johnny would tear a book in half, leaving one part with one farmer and the other with another, and then switch them when he came back through. Nothing gave him greater satisfaction than to discuss and share his "Good News, fresh from Heaven!" Today, we seek to expand the spiritual orchard that Johnny began.

J. Appleseed & Co.

3200 Washington Street
San Francisco, CA 94115

The Country of Spirit, *by Wilson Van Dusen, Ph.D.*

Immediately upon its 1992 release, this volume of selected writings became an instant classic, as Dr. Van Dusen has done once again what he does so well, which is to interpret the depths of Swedenborg's extensive theology and translate it into a compelling approach to spiritual practice for the modern day pilgrim. Included are essays on mysticism, meditation, reincarnation, dream interpretation, and his enormously popular essay on usefulness, plus several others. Exciting reading for the practical seeker.

(132 pages, paperback)
$7 postpaid

Presence of Other Worlds, *by Wilson Van Dusen, Ph.D.*

The leading modern interpretive work on Swedenborg, clinical psychologist and mystic Wilson Van Dusen penetrates the complexities of Swedenborg's singular journey in a way that is helpful particularly for people who are experimental seekers.

"Here is an account of a scientific genius, dead two centuries, who having mastered all that science knew of the external world, went on to a daring, often frightening exploration of the inner world. Van Dusen, having traveled some of the same distance himself, presents Swedenborg sympathetically in the man's own terms. An exciting, thought provoking book which will appeal especially, I believe, to those persons who are not afraid of the inner psychic world." — *Carl Rogers, Author and pioneer in humanistic psychology*

(240 pages, paperback.
Published by the Swedenborg Foundation)
$7 postpaid

To order, please send your check or money order to:
Order Department
J. Appleseed & Co.
3200 Washington Street,
San Francisco, CA 94115
Be sure to specify which books, how many, your name and mailing address.